My COVID Crucible

My COVID Crucible

Living with a Pandemic

George R. Crisp

RESOURCE *Publications* · Eugene, Oregon

MY COVID CRUCIBLE
Living with a Pandemic

Resource Publications
An Imprint of Wipf and Stock Publishers
199 W. 8th Ave., Suite 3
Eugene, OR 97401

www.wipfandstock.com

PAPERBACK ISBN: 978-1-6667-5136-9
HARDCOVER ISBN: 978-1-6667-5137-6
EBOOK ISBN: 978-1-6667-5138-3

12/16/22

With profound appreciation and gratitude, this book is dedicated to ...

... Sue Crisp, my wife, whose compassion, strength, and love were ever-present companions on each step of this journey, faithfully keeping her vow to love me "in sickness and in health." With elevated concern she met every challenge my illness presented. She put her patience and invaluable practical nature to use for my benefit;

... The doctors and nurses who applied their valuable medical knowledge, considerable skill, and empathy to the care of COVID-19 patients everywhere, and notably those medical professionals who cared for me;

... The family, friends, and people who don't know me, for offering their prayers and best wishes for my recovery to good health;

... The national, state and local health officials who advised the public about COVID-19 with sound science, clear messaging, and dedicated concern for our nation during this public health crisis.

Contents

Introduction

THIS IS THE PERSONAL story of my encounter with COVID-19, a story I have been encouraged to relate. It is also a record of my feelings, opinions, and observations of the way I have experienced the virus and how it has affected our common life. This book originated in brief reflections, which I labeled a blog, written while a hospital patient suffering from COVID pneumonia in December of 2020.

My intent is to describe what life was like for me between March 2020 and March 2021. For most of that time I was healthy and physically unaffected by the virus. But for the months of December 2020 and January 2021, life with the virus in my body was harder than I ever could have imagined. Not being able to breathe properly is disconcerting at the least and frightening at the worst.

Writing a memoir such as this is more than an intellectual challenge. Introspection does not come easily to me, especially when it comes to self-exploration. While I enjoy being reflective in poetry or songwriting, I wrestle with what is fair self-disclosure and what is oversharing. For years I have carried a generous ego, but strive to not make myself the story. I hope I have struck a balance with this testimony.

The novel coronavirus known as COVID-19 continues to have a significant impact on life in the United States. Indeed, life all over our planet has been affected by this global pandemic. It has cost millions of lives, strained our health care systems and health care workers at all levels, and altered the fabric of our lives for more than a year.

This public health crisis is so pervasive we've almost become numb to the statistics reported to us on a daily basis. It has been the leading story as the media have covered the number of daily cases, hospitalizations, and deaths. We've heard endless pleas to follow the guidelines of the Centers for Disease Control and Prevention (CDC) and the rationale for doing so. As pharmaceutical giants began to develop vaccines, each step of the process was reported and debated *ad infinitum*. When the vaccines began to roll out, there were distribution challenges, eligibility decisions to be made, and a sense of hopefulness began to emerge.

Fairly or not, the coronavirus has been compared with the 1918 Spanish influenza epidemic, which I briefly learned about in high school history books. I've seen the old photos of uniformed nurses tending to patients in steel-framed beds with curved head- and footboards. But I was alive to experience the COVID crisis and the devastating toll it has taken on many aspects of life. I have witnessed reports of the rising cases, hospitalizations, and deaths that have come with this disease. Thirty, forty, or fifty years from now, this era will be in the history books for others to learn. You may remember how you experienced this phenomenon, but it may be novel information for future readers.

In a noticeably brief time, COVID-19 became a disease handled as a political problem, not simply a public health crisis. With divisive national elections, the beginnings of a long-overdue racial reckoning, and various cultural clashes, it became clear that we are a deeply divided nation. Senseless violence against Asian-Americans, public demonstrations providing some with excuses for vandalism and looting, and the sinful ugliness of white supremacy all contributed to the tumult of 2020.

The pandemic brought hardships through job losses, food insecurity, housing crises, and a crushing blow to the health care industry. These issues led to economic uncertainty not seen since the Great Recession (2008) or the Great Depression (1930s). COVID-19 exposed serious gaps in the health care system, especially among low-income workers and people of color.

> *Note: Interspersed in my text are COVID tracking statistics indicating new cases each month and the cumulative number of deaths for the thirteen months covered in this volume. These are figures from the World Health Organization, posted on Wikipedia and accessed June 12, 2021.*

Yale Medicine published a clever hypodermic needle graphic—"Our Pandemic Year—A COVID-19 Timeline"—on March 9, 2021. (The graphic can be viewed at https://www.yalemedicine.org/news/covid-timeline.) It charts the appearance of a mysterious new illness, the rapid spread of the virus, and the months when the world shut down. Then came the summer uptick in mental health issues as people struggled, a new sense of hope with the emergency authorization of two vaccines, and the decline of cases and deaths.

There are many others who will write about the coronavirus and the associated matters I chronicle. They will be more polished or professional as journalists or social critics; they will utilize better resources and data-bases or conduct interviews with health care experts. Their dissection and evaluations may be more detailed and complete than mine. What will be written about COVID-19 is sure to be more eloquent in describing the big picture of this pandemic time.

Yusef Salaam, a wrongly accused and later exonerated member of the Central Park Five is the author of *Better Not Bitter: Living on Purpose in the Pursuit of Racial Justice*. Recently interviewed on the TODAY show,[1] he mentioned something which touched my heart. He said, "I want people to understand that when you go through a trial, when you are tested, then you can testify. You have a testimony to make because you were able to grow through something not just go through something."

This is my personal take on the experience of living through this year, having contracted the disease known as COVID pneumonia, and surviving. This is a trial through which I have been tested, and I want to testify. I hope I have grown through this experience. I grieve with those whose loved ones have died, and I rejoice in the blessing of being alive to write.

1. Craig Melvin, TODAY, May 18, 2021.

1

A Dawning Awareness

THE WIDESPREAD ENGLISH EXPRESSION, "May you live in interesting times," is said to be a translation of a Chinese curse, although there is no definitive source for it in Chinese culture. This statement is often used ironically to evoke a sense of blessing with a hint of caution. Contemporary time is quite interesting, and learning what to do with what confronts us on any given day is part of the art of living.

In a similar way, it is frequently said that the Chinese word for "crisis" contains the characters for "danger" and "opportunity." Notable people such as President John F. Kennedy, Vice President Al Gore, and Secretary of State Condoleezza Rice used this trope in their speeches. Its widespread use indicates the popularity of this idea, especially when faced with a crisis. What we do in a crisis reveals our collective character and resolve to work through the issues before us.

While neither of these concepts is truly rooted in Chinese language and culture, they provide food for thought as we have coped with the COVID-19 public health crisis. This disease has become a part of our collective consciousness. How we have responded to it is a matter of public debate. What effect it has had on our social fabric will continue to be revealed.

My first awareness of the virus was a November 2019 news report of a cluster of viral pneumonia cases discovered in Wuhan, People's Republic of China. The World Health Organization first officially reported this on

December 31, 2019.[1] There was vague speculation that it had been found in a wet market and was likely transmitted from an animal to a human. Not much else was known about the virus at that time. It was reported to be a severe acute respiratory syndrome (SARS) virus, and scientists were monitoring it. It was one of those news stories that caught my interest but not my full attention, so I put it in the back of my mind.

Unbeknown to me, however, almost immediately, scientists went to work to identify this "mysterious pneumonia-like illness" by decoding its genetic sequence. Was it "a known pathogen or something entirely new?" Using equipment made in the United States, an Illumina sequencing machine, the genetic code of the virus was identified by January 10, 2020. In a record time of twenty days, the engineers at biotech Moderna developed a vaccine to fight the virus, lightning speed for the biotech world.[2] This was possible, in part, because of scientific breakthroughs in genetic sequencing. Still, it took nearly a year to move from developing the vaccine to making it widely available.

The following month, news outlets began reporting possible connections between travel and the virus, leading to travel restrictions for people from China, or those who had recently visited there. The idea, of course, was to limit further exposure to the highly contagious virus. Given the tensions between the United States and China, the caution did not seem out of the ordinary.

After the first of the year, the first case in the United States hit the news. As I recall, a person from the state of Washington became infected. (The first U.S. case was reported on January 20, 2020.) In February 2020, news outlets reported the first death from the virus in the U.S.

By this time, the World Health Organization (WHO) had given the virus a name: COVID-19, short for **Co**rona **VI**rus **D**isease, 2019. The official date of this designation was February 11, 2020, according to the Centers for Disease Control (CDC). It was so named "to enable discussion on disease prevention, spread, transmissibility, severity and treatment," as noted by the WHO.[3] With each new day, reports of cases and deaths from this virus were on the rise, and a sense of anxiety developed. On March 11, the W.H.O. declared the coronavirus outbreak a global pandemic."[4] *Webster's Dictionary*

1. WHO, December 31, 2019.
2. Park, "Decoding COVID-19," 57.
3. World Health Organization website accessed April 9, 2021.
4. Taylor, "Coronavirus and Epidemic or Pandemic?"

defines a pandemic as a disease outbreak "occurring over a wide geographic area and affecting an exceptionally high proportion of the population."[5]

The Director-General of the World Health Organization, Dr. Tedros Adhanom Ghebreyesus, at a March 11, 2020, briefing, noted that the WHO is "assessing the outbreak around the clock." He expressed concern about the "alarming levels of spread and severity, and by the alarming levels of inactivity." Saying he doesn't use the word pandemic lightly, Dr. Ghebreyesus added, "This is the first pandemic caused by a coronavirus."[6]

COVID TRACKING—March 2020
Cases: 62 / Deaths: 1

Some statistics to consider—at the end of 2020, Johns Hopkins reported there had been more than five hundred and sixty thousand deaths in the United States. The U.S. had 34.1 million cases, one-fourth of the world's cases. The CDC has confirmed that COVID-19 became the third leading cause of death in 2020, behind heart disease and cancer according to a National Public Radio report.[7] On February 23, 2021, the Associated Press noted the COVID-19 death toll in the U.S. has matched the number of Americans killed in World War II, the Korean War, and the Vietnam war combined.[8]

At first, it seemed that COVID-19 was attacking those who had recently traveled, or residents of nursing homes and convalescent facilities. It appeared the elderly and those with underlying health conditions were the most vulnerable to the disease. In time, this proved to be only a partially accurate hypothesis, as younger people also were affected. It was also suggested the virus was spread through contact with un-sanitized surfaces, rather than the airborne illness it proved to be.

The Centers for Disease Control and Prevention (CDC) advised Americans to wash their hands frequently and properly. The idea of social distancing at an interval of six feet was introduced, and mask wearing strongly recommended. These mitigation efforts were aimed at preventing the spread of this growing public health crisis. It was not difficult to add these measures to my daily routine, and it was curious to see how other people reacted with either compliance or resistance.

5 *Webster's*, s.v. "pandemic," 850.

6. Ghebreyesus, https://www.who.int/director-general /speeches.

7. NPR, March 31, 2021.

8. Associated Press, February 23, 2021.

The number of cases climbed; the death rate continued to increase. Hospitals were soon overrun with patients. The demand for personal protective equipment (PPE) increased and was soon in short supply. In the context of COVID-19, PPE specifically included gloves, N-95 medical masks, eye protection, gowns, aprons, and close-toed shoes.[9]

The CDC published the following list of symptoms and they were quickly posted in a wide range of places. "People with these symptoms may have COVID-19:

- Fever or chills

- Cough

- Shortness of breath or difficulty breathing

- Fatigue

- Muscle or body aches

- Headache

- New loss of taste or smell

- Sore throat

- Congestion or runny nose

- Nausea or vomiting

- Diarrhea"[10]

This list does not include all possible symptoms, and cases ranged from mild symptoms to severe illness. Older adults and people who have severe underlying medical conditions like heart or lung disease or diabetes seem to be at higher risk for developing more serious complications from COVID-19 illness.

The CDC was also quick to publish guidelines for the prevention of COVID-19.[11] This is a simplified list, but the CDC's guidelines were quite detailed:

- Wear a mask to cover your nose and mouth.

- Stay six feet away from others.

9. health.com, accessed April 9, 2021.

10. cdc.gov, accessed June 23, 2021.

11. cdc.gov, accessed June 23, 2021.

- Wash your hands often with soap and water or use a hand sanitizer with at least 60 percent alcohol.

- Avoid touching your nose and mouth.

- Cover coughs and sneezes.

- Clean and disinfect high touch surfaces daily.

- Monitor your health daily; take your temperature and be alert for symptoms.

City, county, and state public health departments kept the populace informed as we watched the spread of COVID-19 in our area. San Bernardino County officials refused to release statistical numbers about the virus in our area until we reached the 100 deaths mark. Plans for a lockdown grew louder and were eventually ordered. All non-essential workers were advised to work from home, and people were advised to avoid unnecessary driving. (Essential workers included doctors and nurses, grocery store and gas station employees, police and other first responders, and a host of curiously selected workers.)

> **COVID TRACKING—April 2020**
> **Cases: 213,199 / Deaths: 3,155**

Soon, state and local authorities implemented a general "shelter in place," stay-at-home strategy. The dawning awareness of the danger of the coronavirus, and how seriously we needed to follow these precautionary measures, began to sink into the mind of the public. A steadily increasing number of citizens started to follow the suggestions and mandates.

The daily barrage of news coverage became exhausting for me. The statistics were multiplying faster than my brain could process them. Reports of the staggering number of deaths added grief and sadness to my days. I realized it was necessary to inform the public about this public health crisis, but the significance of this disease became oppressive.

When the coronavirus crisis began, we were just two weeks into the Christian season of Lent, and for many of us it began to feel like the longest Lenten season ever. (For the non-religious, it might have seemed like a long time-out.) While Lent draws us closer to the cross, COVID-19 was beginning to feel like a prolonged Good Friday.

Lent is traditionally a season in which people choose a spiritual discipline—giving something up or taking something on (or both), a practical discipline of forgoing chocolate, sweets or caffeine, or spiritual exercises of prayer, study or self-giving—as a way of drawing closer to God. This crisis was a discipline we did not choose. The "COVID Lent" did not feel all that spiritual. Given the two- to three-week incubation period of the virus, I hoped it would be largely behind us by Easter. It wasn't.

In a seasonal metaphor, with COVID-19 we entered a long, dark winter. Southern California winters are generally mild, but I've had some experience with persistent freezing temperatures in other locations. One does not casually venture into the cold without a great deal of preparation, if only to shovel the sidewalk after a snowstorm. The bare trees and gray skies can mute the sunniest of dispositions. Winter makes it easy to withdraw into the cozy confines of an easy chair or into my own thoughts and feelings. The joke in such winter climates is that you are either living through winter, preparing for it, or recovering from it.

This COVID winter didn't send me to the coat closet, neither did I retreat into the darker places of my interior life. It provided me with copious time for reflection and creativity. Each day was an invitation to pursue my interests and figure out ways to express myself. At the same time, I was aware of how some of my friends were becoming anxious and depressed when their activities became so limited.

The social distancing and lockdown orders felt like a forced hibernation. Despite the warmth of spring, the heat of summer, or the cooling transition of the fall, each day seemed to prolong the chilly winter atmosphere. It was a feeling neither Zoom nor FaceTime could dispel, even if they lifted the gloom temporarily.

I can't remember exactly when it first appeared in my daily newspaper, but they started printing a Coronavirus Daily Tracker with statistics, charts and graphs containing data about COVID-19 in our region.[12] The Tracker provided a constant and comprehensive record of information of how and where the virus was progressing. It traced data by age, ethnicity, and percentage of the population, and contained statistics by county, nation, and world's top ten countries by cases.

This daily report had graphs showing the trends in cases, hospitalizations, and deaths. As the crisis continued, the Tracker added information about testing rates (replacing recoveries) as well as the number and percentage of the population who had received vaccinations. In addition to this print-medium reporting, there were also daily televised briefings by big

12. Goertzen and Snibbe, Tracker.

city mayors and state governors, keeping the citizenry informed of how our government authorities were managing this health crisis.

Initially, I would study the Tracker with great interest, comparing our city and county with other areas of the state. I decided to focus on the most positive statistic they were reporting, one that the electronic media was *not* reporting: the number of recoveries from COVID-19. This statistic revealed how recoveries outnumbered the deaths from the virus at the rate of four to one.

Eventually, I could not absorb the flood of information that was presented and the Tracker became an afterthought for me, a page in the paper I would glide past without a second glance. Only on occasion, when I wanted a particular stat to sink in, would I pore over the page to glean the information. The Tracker was all too real and overwhelming as it traced trends in new daily cases, hospitalizations and deaths.

As time passed and the two-week quarantine extended, our phone conversations with family and friends involved inquiries about our activities during the lockdown. Young people offered to run errands or grocery shop for their elders, including my wife Sue and me. We were touched when a young couple of our church reached out to us to make such an offer. We politely declined as we were fending for ourselves without difficulty.

With the virus came a new set of words and phrases we began to use. We developed a jargon to help us communicate, cope with, and joke about COVID-19. While in quarantine, we learned how to spell quarantine. Among the first puns I heard was the word "quarantini," which was a general reference to cocktails at home. That was followed by puns using the Corona beer brand (e.g., "I got Corona today"). It wasn't long before other coronavirus jokes began to circulate. Two examples:

- I'll tell you a coronavirus joke now, but you'll have to wait two weeks to see if you got it.
- Since we're all in quarantine, I guess we'll be making only inside jokes from now on.

On the serious side, we started using phrases like "shelter in place," "stay at home," or "lockdown." We were "social distancing." Public health officials asked us to help "flatten the curve" and "slow the spread" of the virus. Even as the cases increased, we heard, "We are all in this together," intended as encouraging and sustaining words. The phrase "social isolation" appeared, which sounded like an oxymoron to me.

Wearing masks became commonplace, mandated in many places, and we learned which masks were the most effective. N-95 masks were considered the most effective, but we were urged to save them for medical personnel. Some people rejected wearing a mask as an infringement of their personal freedom. Reasonable people saw mask-wearing as both a self-protective practice and an expression of care for those around them. Mask-making became an outlet for creative fabric artists who made decorative masks in many themes to appeal to our interests and hobbies, show support for our favorite sports teams, or reflect our professions or our sense of humor.

Masks were an easy item to add to daily habits. They were relatively inexpensive—often provided for free. Masks were effective at slowing the spread of the virus and we would wear them out of love and concern for others as well as for our own health and self-protection. Sadly, some people felt like the mask mandates were a form of crowd control that impinged on their freedom. I was baffled by what people didn't get about mask-wearing as a way to mitigate a public health crisis.

The coronavirus was relentless, and in time we were talking about "COVID testing" and "contact tracing" along with the lingo that comes with those ideas. Making testing kits available and administering them, with an unpleasant deep swab of the nose, was a part of our learning curve. There was also a period, early on, when therapeutic treatment options to help COVID-19 patients were bandied about before the medical experts— virologists, epidemiologists and pulmonary physicians—settled on the most effective drugs. In addition, pharmaceutical companies were pressed to develop vaccines and we learned what that process involves. Testing the safety and effectiveness of vaccines happened on an accelerated basis. These efforts at tackling the coronavirus pandemic, addressing it from various angles, came with new bits of language which soon permeated our lives.

Another aspect of our education came from various public health organizations. Our awareness of the CDC, the National Institutes of Health (NIH), and the WHO brought all those acronyms into our daily lives. The spokespeople from those institutions became household names—Dr. Anthony Fauci, Dr. Deborah Brix, and Dr. Francis Collins, to name just a few. I would see them nearly every day as they were interviewed on televised news shows. Also, state and local health officials, some whose names were not widely known, were called upon to inform the public via the daily news briefings conducted by mayors and governors.

COVID TRACKING—May 2020
Cases: 1,035,353 / Deaths: 61,347

As COVID deaths were mounting, the calamity of this virus was more dramatically brought home to me as reporters broadcast the news of refrigerator trucks being used as makeshift morgues, storing the bodies of the deceased. To make matters worse, people were dying in isolation with no contact from family members or loved ones in their final moments. Doctors and nurses heroically served as agents of compassion while human life slipped away.

With coronavirus cases, hospitalizations, and deaths increasing came awareness of the health care workers on the front lines providing crucial medical care. Every evening I would see news reports of emergency room and intensive care unit doctors and nurses who were working long shifts with inadequate equipment to care for the sick and dying. They were often isolated from family members to avoid infecting them with some pathogen brought home from the hospital. Some of those medical professionals quarantined themselves to a portion of their house, a garage, or a motorhome in their driveway.

At some point the recognition of their dedication and sacrifice found its way into the public consciousness. For a week or two, maybe longer, the public was encouraged to go outside at 7:00 p.m. and bang pots and pans, make some noise, to honor these medical heroes. I participated in this display once but could not see any lasting benefit. This recognition was extended to emergency medical technicians, police, and fire departments, and other first responders who were potentially at risk for doing their jobs. Handmade "Hero" and "Thank You" signs started appearing in the area around hospitals. Pizzas, cookies and other food were delivered to medical personnel in gratitude for their hard work and courage in the face of this crisis.

Before long, it was clear that COVID was here to stay, and Sue and I made the necessary adjustments in our lifestyle to accommodate the situation. This meant fewer errands to run, more phone contact with relatives and friends, and more quiet days at home with only merchandise deliveries to disturb our domestic tranquility. But we were far from idle.

2

The Lockdown Experience

IN THE INITIAL PHASE of the COVID lockdown, the government authorities directed us to isolate ourselves for two weeks. A two-week lockdown is something you ride out, and most people were cooperative, thinking this would pass quickly and we'd get back to life as usual. Officials were calling this a public health crisis and describing the urgency of the situation. We watched as the virus spread. As the crisis deepened, and cases became hospitalizations, it became clear that we were in an unusual situation which required patience and willing participation. At this point there still seemed to be a sense of common purpose.

Early on, when restaurants were still open, some COVID rules were put in place to reduce people's exposure to the virus. Salt, pepper, sugar and condiments were removed, tables were taken away or separated to limit seating, and fountain drink dispensers were no longer available for customer use. Many restaurants shifted to take-out orders, and fast-food places became drive through only. Delivery services like Grub Hub, Door Dash and Postmates expanded their businesses as people began sheltering in place. The simple pleasure of dining out was being taken away by COVID.

In the early days of the pandemic, the only shopping Sue and I did was to resupply our home with a week's worth of groceries. There were special hours for seniors to shop, and some stores restricted the number of customers allowed in at one time. Employees with counters would stand at the door and keep track. We bought basic supplies of milk, fruits and vegetables, canned goods and bread. We added modest amounts of frozen food, meat, and dry goods. Almost immediately, paper goods were cleared off the shelves, frustrating us as we shopped for those products. If items were on the shelf, we made sure we had paper towels, toilet paper, napkins and facial tissues. We did not see the need to hoard anything but were practical enough to pick up items we could store for later use when we saw them on the shelf.

Cleaning products, disinfectants, soap, alcohol and bleach were hard to come by. After an initial wave of purchases emptied the shelves, the stores could not keep these items in stock. The stores blamed the delivery system or the distributors. The delivery people pointed fingers at the manufacturers and the producers pushed the blame game down the road to the suppliers. The media broadcast shameful, appalling stories of farmers destroying crops and dumping milk because the distribution systems had broken down. In addition, meat packing plants were hit hard by the number of their employees testing positive for COVID-19.

Grocery store employees sanitized the shopping carts, maintained social distancing, had one-way aisles that most people ignored, and required facial coverings which many people did not wear properly. ("I have COPD," was a common excuse.) Because of those people who did stockpile key products, stores began to limit the number of particular items one could buy. Although we were used to recycling our own shopping bags, we were also called upon to bag our own groceries. This was when the public health experts were concerned about contact spreading the virus and before proclaiming that COVID was a respiratory, airborne pathogen. We were also encouraged to sanitize our groceries once we brought them home. Eventually, some of these practices were eased and a greater sense of normalcy returned to the shopping experience.

The rapidity of these changes was stressful to some, and in some respects, they shut down any interaction with all but a small number of other people. Some people were easy-going and accepting; they made jokes and tried to be pleasant through all the circumstances everyone was experiencing. There were those who grumbled or rebelled as they grudgingly adopted this new set of rules. Others were more philosophical about all these things, aware that a mask doesn't have to limit pleasant human interaction. My sense was that Sue and I were rolling with the punches brought about by these changes.

For me, one of the first casualties of COVID-19 was the closure of the churches. Redlands First United Methodist Church (UMC), our home church for the previous seven years, suspended in-person worship on March 15. Two weeks earlier, I had been the guest preacher at Banning UMC, the third guest preaching opportunity I had as the year began. While we initially thought the church closures would be temporary, it became clear they would be extended. This meant no more preaching opportunities were on the horizon, and we suddenly had nowhere to go on Sunday mornings.

Especially disappointing for me was the loss of a guest preaching spot at Trinity Episcopal Church which had been set up for May 3. I had been attending Trinity once a month for about two years and had been added to their "Preaching Rota." I was honored to be invited to let out the "closet Episcopalian" side of me. The date had been of my choosing—Good Shepherd Sunday, the fourth Sunday after Easter—a week with a solid theme in the Revised Common Lectionary. Reluctantly, I phoned the rector to ask about rescheduling.

The pandemic brought about a quick but difficult shift to online worship for many churches as pastors were forced to switch to electronic media to reach their socially isolated congregations. Some pastors found it easy to begin live streaming modified services with a reduced number of worship leaders. Others took to pre-recording parts of the service and editing the results for broadcasting via Zoom, FaceTime or other platforms, in order to meet the spiritual needs of the people.

The simplest approach was to replicate worship services online, keeping the liturgy as familiar as possible. More innovative leaders developed new liturgies to fit the media platform they had available. There arose an immediate and vigorous debate over how to celebrate the Eucharist, and whether to do so at all.

As many colleagues told me, a worship team was organized to manage various aspects of presenting worship online. I learned that someone was needed to operate the broadcasting and recording equipment. A team of musicians developed and presented hymns and service music. Either a roster of worship leaders (liturgists) or a selected individual managed those responsibilities. In congregations with young families, some form of a children's ministry was offered to engage the youngest disciples. Of course, the clergy offered leadership in preaching, praying and encouraging the community of faith who tuned in each week. I witnessed many of these approaches as I tuned in to "attend" their services.

Whether led by a select few or a wide spectrum of church members, the notion of worship online began to lose its appeal for me. I came to think of it as "two-dimensional church." Given the opportunity to tune in at the designated worship time or at a time of my own choosing, I found more interesting things to do with my Sunday morning than *observe* church.

Elements of worship were there, but I was missing the warm presence of people with whom I could interact. For me, what makes the church experience even more valuable than the music, the Scripture and the word duly preached, is the animating presence of the people, the body of Christ, who are the essence of the church. Watching worship is clearly different from embodied worship with others.

As more and more of my colleagues adapted to some form of online worship, I listened to as many as five sermons each week. I eventually fell into a pattern of listening to one or two sermons, rotating among the services my colleagues offered. I was also able to see colleagues in other parts of the country as they led worship.

Soon after this national health crisis was declared, my siblings in the Order of Saint Luke (OSL, or the Order) took action.[1] Understanding the value of community, and knowing that meeting together would not be possible, OSL members wrote "A Liturgy for When We Cannot Meet."[2] Acknowledging the distance between people, and the pain and suffering being experienced, this liturgy used scriptural references and four symbolic gestures—lighting a candle, holding a Bible, drinking water, and eating a piece of bread—to celebrate God's presence with us in difficult times. Since the end of March 2020, a faithful group of OSL members has prayed this service together every week.

The California-Pacific Chapter of the Order began to hold Evening Prayer services on March 18. At first we met via Zoom on Wednesday and Friday evenings but reduced our meetings to Wednesdays after a couple of weeks. Using materials published by OSL, we have prayed together through the liturgical seasons with hymns, psalms and Scripture lessons befitting the occasion. A solid group of our chapter has been quite faithful to this spiritual discipline. Later in the year we learned that several other OSL chapters were meeting via Zoom, as we were, to pray various daily offices. Despite the pandemic, OSL members have stayed faithful to their vow to pray the Daily Office. The Daily Office is a series of liturgical prayer services

1. See www.saint-luke.net.
2. Fender, Beth et. al., "A Liturgy for When We Cannot Meet."

held at particular times of the day, but it may also refer to a time of intentional personal devotions.

Another casualty of the pandemic for me was the cancellation of the OSL spring Council meeting. It had been scheduled for May 2020 at the Franciscan Renewal Center in Scottsdale, Arizona. In place of a Council meeting, we organized a series of worship services on Zoom to resemble the worship we would have had if we were meeting. We agreed not to conduct any business but only worship together. Others in the Order were invited to participate. We asked OSL leaders to submit a written report of the activities of their work area, but all other business was either put in abeyance or left for the general officers' discernment.

Another group I belong to also shifted gears in the face of COVID. My Lectionary Study Group (LSG), which has met for several years, is basically a Bible study for preachers. Individuals take turns leading a discussion of the Scripture passages of the Lectionary, giving focus to the passage he or she plans to use for preaching. There is ample respect and camaraderie among the group members. We normally met four times a year for a study retreat but could no longer meet face-to-face and took to Zoom for our study sessions. We adjusted to a once-a-week meeting, and in place of presenting six to eight lessons per session we began to present one or two. Instead of working several weeks in advance, we had a shorter window of two to three weeks. We also engaged in casual conversation, sharing our individual experiences during the pandemic and keeping abreast of the news in our Annual Conference. The Annual Conference is the basic organizational body in in the United Methodist Church. It includes both lay and ministerial members of all United Methodist churches in a geographically defined area, in our case southern California, Hawaii, Guam and Saipan.

A weekly pattern of Zoom calls on Sundays, Tuesdays and Wednesdays became part of my routine. After a while, these meetings became so habitual I no longer noted them on my calendar. Occasionally, a Zoom meeting was added to this mix, mostly OSL gatherings of some kind. I participated in an online Easter Vigil service, a Marian Feast, an Ascension service, and later in the year an All Saints' service. The pandemic protocols may have altered our practices, but they did not diminish the vibrancy of the OSL community.

My feelings about OSL worship derive from my forty-year association with the charism of the Order and some deeply spiritual experiences I've had within that community. Being a member in the Order has enriched my ministry and grounded me in liturgical worship. Especially when I have needed it, the Order has provided spiritual renewal and sustained my faith. My local church connections are meaningful, but they have had a briefer "shelf life" than those with my OSL siblings. I'm sure I have invested myself in the Order in a way different than I have with my professional appointments. Our liturgically- and sacramentally-minded Order has found a way to worship together, even if two-dimensional worship is less than ideal.

Trying to describe the role or meaning of the Order in my life is challenging. Well-developed liturgy has always had an allure for me, and through the Order I have learned the elements of worship that elevate my spirit and stretch my soul. Liturgy is the framework on which I build a meaningful encounter with God through prayers, song, Scripture, and the sacraments. The gathered community, or the individual in devotion, can draw near to God with a familiar pattern of worship. The Order has helped me mine the riches of our faith tradition to experience this enhanced expression of integrity in worship.

The OSL community has been the richest source of spiritual companionship and demanding theological reflection. The Order has been a wellspring of thoughtful, provocative and inspirational experiences. The printed resources alone have fueled my ministry, and knowing the authors of the material in our publications has deepened my appreciation.

In the Order, we covenant to live a sacramental life. I see that as allowing the deeper meanings of baptism and Eucharist to permeate not just a ritual act but every fiber of my being. To see the sacred in the ordinary and the ordinary in the sacred has become a fundamental value for me. Water, wheat and wine are practical, physical elements, but the new life and forgiveness they symbolize echo far beyond the moment of their application. The sacraments are life-changing moments of connection and peace that bring me closer to Jesus than anything I can imagine.

Not long after government agencies began instituting coronavirus protocols, winter gave way to spring, and hopes emerged for an end to the lockdown. The prospect of warmer weather made people long for outdoor activities, but the virus cases did not let up. Weeks of confinement at home were making people edgy.

By Memorial Day weekend, large, unprotected gatherings happened, making news by their defiance of the rules. The motorcycle rally in Sturgis, South Dakota, college parties, holiday gatherings and political rallies are a few examples. In my opinion, two factors led to these superspreader events.

First, folks tired of COVID-19 sequestering craved social contact. Second, there was a freedom debate and a defiance of the government encroaching on people's "rights." Both factors are weak excuses for flouting advisories in a public health crisis.

With the lockdown continuing beyond almost every-one's expectations, the social seclusion was taking a toll. As a musician, I particularly appreciated how many performers stepped in to ease the isolation. In certain situations, solo musicians would open their doors and windows to entertain the folks in other apartments or homes. A few artists quickly used the internet to release COVID-related videos: Neil Diamond released a "Sweet Caroline" remake with the lyrics: "Hands, washing hands . . ." Neil Young with Crazy Horse put out "Shut It Down 2020," interspersed with images from the daily news of the pandemic.

With entertainment venues shut down, some artists began live streaming music for their fans. A famous example is Andrea Bocelli's twenty-five-minute "Music for Hope" Easter concert, live from the beautiful Duomo di Milano on April 12, 2020. In his introductory voice-over (in Italian), Bocelli said, "Thanks to music streamed live, bringing together millions of clasped hands everywhere in the world, we will hug this wounded world's pulsing heart."[3] The performance included the classic 1872 composition Panis Angelicus ("bread of angels"), written by César Franck for his *Messe á tres voix.* Hearing this selection was quite moving for me, as this composition has been in my repertoire for nearly fifty years. Standing on the gentle sloping steps of the cathedral, Bocelli ended with the folk hymn "Amazing Grace."

☙⎯◈⎯❧

The news was full of stories about other creative expressions, more personal, low-key, and family-centered of how people coped with the pandemic. Bread-making, all sorts of baking, and home cooking occupied people's time and attention while staying at home. When stuck at home, for whatever reason, life can develop into a tedious routine. Get up and dressed (or stay in your jammies), eat breakfast and then do *something*—read the paper, check your email, deal with a task of your choice or maybe tackle a major project. Stop for lunch and then do something else—surprise the kids, watch television, call a friend. The day wears on and you make dinner, catch the evening news, put the kids to bed, read a book, shower, and go to

---

3. YouTube, May 21, 2021.

bed. You get up the next morning and repeat, and again the day after, and the day after that, and so on *ad infinitum.*

None of this was exactly my daily schedule, but I had my mundane moments. For me, any variation to the routine is a welcome distraction. I believe it is helpful to be intentional about bringing some structure to life; be mindful and self-motivated and the time will fly by. With social isolation being pressed upon us all, mental health can suffer, depression can set in, and feelings of self-worth can take a beating. Human beings are social creatures, after all. I held off those feelings by having a sense of purpose each day.

During the pandemic people became hungry for human connection, longing for hugs, handshakes, and eye-to-eye communication. Introverts may have relished the isolation and quiet time. The seclusion may have been welcome at first but might also lead to loneliness. The lack of interaction may have stymied extroverts or energized them to find other means of communication. I am fairly balanced on the introvert-extrovert scale. I welcome time for reflection and creativity, but I'm also energized by interaction with a variety of people. When isolation becomes tedious, I seek the interactions of social gatherings and vice versa.

Cleaning Steve's Apartment

By accident, just as everything was shutting down, Sue and I took on a big project to help a friend. It gave us something meaningful to do when we were wondering how we would deal with the imposed social isolation. Steve Brendza, the brother of our friend Bob Brendza, died on March 2, 2020, just as the nation was coming to grips with the virus. (To my knowledge he did not have COVID.) When I called Bob to express my sympathy, he asked if I wanted a guitar that belonged to Steve. Although I wasn't in the market for a new guitar, I agreed to evaluate it. Steve's one-bedroom apartment was in the northern part of San Bernardino, about fifteen miles away.

One of Steve's friends, a high school friend named John, who had recently become a part of Steve's life again, so I scheduled my arrival for a time when John would also be there. At the appointed time, I arrived and met John. After chatting a bit, I looked around at the dismaying scene before me.

Steve had been gone for only a few days, and he had a cat living on its own in the apartment. John had taken responsibility for setting out food and water for the cat and cleaning its litter box. On the day I arrived, that last chore had not yet been done and there was kitty litter spread around the bathroom floor. The odor was strong and I was glad I was wearing a mask. What a quite a mess!

Steve's apartment was dusty and cluttered with many objects that reflected Steve's interests. The kitchen was hardly a place to prepare food; it was more like a makeshift hobby shop. Model airplane kits, paint and glue, tools and lamps covered almost every surface. Outdated staples were stored in the cupboards, growing older by the minute, and the refrigerator held odd containers of food.

A stereo component system occupied an entire corner of what would be the small dining area, along with speakers, guitar amplifiers, lamps of various kinds, and about three hundred CDs, all covered with a thick layer of dust and grime. The area also had an upright piano and two electronic keyboards positioned for easy access. Amid these items I found two acoustic guitars, six electric guitars, and one bass guitar. I evaluated the two acoustic guitars, and I did not think they were worth the cost of cleaning up and rehabilitating.

Elsewhere, I found a case filled with science fiction books, indiscriminate stacks of computer items, and a cable TV and DVD set-up. Almost everywhere I looked I could see fishing equipment of all sorts. From the new or almost new appearance of the fishing tackle, I surmised that this was a recent interest of Steve's. As I was later to discover, several unopened Amazon packages contained fishing gear, and I felt sad that Steve never got to see or use what he had bought.

The details of Steve's life outlived him and were left for Sue and me to discover. In moments like this, I wonder what will become of the treasures I will leave behind some day. Who will have the task of sorting through my possessions and deciding what is valuable and what is junk? What will I leave unfinished, unopened, or unresolved?

The lesson of cleaning Steve's apartment for me is more than "get your affairs in order." Doing this work reminded me of my own mortality and made me think about what the remainders of my life will represent. What non-material things do I value? What kind example have I been to my family and friends? Do my loved ones know how much they mean to me? Have I lived a life that reflects the love I have received and the gifts I have been given? What impact or influence has my being a person of faith, in my case a Christian, had on those around me? These are intangible questions, but rich for reflection and maybe even discussions with friends and family.

My guitar evaluation mission complete, I prepared to say goodbye to John. While I checked out Steve's apartment and possessions, John had a polite but cautious conversation about Steve and his friendship with John. I had been there for little more than an hour, but it was obvious that a great deal of work needed to be done to clear out the space.

I was not eager to take on the task, but Sue and I wanted to help our friend Bob with the aftermath of his brother's death. Bob now lives in Fort Worth, Texas, and could not be on site to oversee the work. Sue spoke with him and volunteered us to clean out the apartment. Bob would arrange with the property manager for us to use a key, and also gave us permission to take anything we wanted.

A few days later we returned to sort through Steve's belongings. We tossed what was plainly broken beyond repair, along with expired food and over-the-counter medications. After four hours we had barely scratched the surface. On subsequent occasions we worked to salvage anything of possible value. We filled our cars with numerous items, but threw damaged things in the dumpster, with a sense of sorrow in our hearts for the lamentable conditions we were finding. The work certainly kept our minds off the pandemic crisis, even as we struggled to breathe beneath our masks on those hot days.

Steve's usable clothing became part of Sue's Trunk Ministry—especially jeans, T-shirts, and tennis shoes. We collected a fair number of tools and at least one toolbox. We brought home whatever appeared to have garage sale value and packed it into our garage for a sale later in the year. We also loaded up with the clothes, shoes and hygiene supplies Sue was collecting.

In the end, Sue and I claimed hundreds of items from Steve's apartment.

Use of Time

During this season of social distancing, many people cleaned closets, dresser drawers, garages and storage units. The gardeners among us worked to beautify their yards and flower beds, and some planted vegetable gardens in hope of a bountiful summer. The more skilled and adventurous took on long-delayed home repair and improvement projects. To avoid going stir-crazy with cabin fever, folks were finding constructive ways to utilize their time. Not being skilled at repair person projects, nor overly ambitious, I kept busy in other self-focused activities. Sue planted a small garden with a minimum of help from me.

People with a different focus decided this was a good time to binge-watch popular shows on their premium media services. Some found comfort in watching old movies. With film and television production companies shut down, network television executives were patch-working their schedules to keep viewers. My entertainment options were limited to network television and programs I recorded to watch on my own schedule.

Movie theaters closed so that particular avenue of entertainment was unavailable, which also meant that my monthly Movie Lovers fellowship group came to an end. Those families with children turned their focus toward more quality family time with board games, craft projects, creating sidewalk chalk messages, or other stay-at-home activities to keep everyone engaged. Parks, beaches and trails were closed even though these outdoor areas provide healthy space to exercise. These things either did not apply or were of no interest to me, but every day was busy with some endeavor that kept me going.

In February and early March, I was busy in my friend Dave's Harmony recording studio, putting the finishing touches on my *Beautiful Day* CD. Dave and I did our last recording session four days after the churches closed, and the same day that COVID restrictions went into effect—just under the wire. I had already arranged for Paul Svenson, a friend of more than fifty years, to master the album, and I needed to get the tracks recorded and sent to him. This was accomplished and the album completed, manufactured, and sent back to me, the proud artist with no place to market my latest product.

My Quarantine Bookshelf

One of the pluses of being in a lockdown situation is catching up on your reading, either with books you planned to read or with books that catch your interest when you discover them. I had started reading the books on my list before the pandemic, but my quarantine bookshelf got a kickstart after cleaning out Steve's apartment. Two books on his bookshelf wound up in my hands as part of the items I claimed.

Another pair of books came from selections I made on Audible, the online audio and podcast service owned by Amazon. After listening to both books, I bought hard copies and actually read them. One book was a gift and another pair of books were by an author I encountered via Zoom.

Here is my quarantine bookshelf (in alphabetical order by author, not the order in which I read them):

Fleetwood Mac: The First 30 Years—Bob Brunning

White Fragility: Why It's So Hard for White People to Talk About Racism—Robin DiAngelo

The Council of Dads—Bruce Feiler

Lennon in America—Geoffrey Giuliano

My Israel Trail: Finding Peace in the Promised Land—Aryeh Greene

Here Comes the Sun: the Spiritual and Musical Journey of George Harrison—Joshua M. Greene

Lightfoot—Nicholas Jennings

Me—Elton John

All You Need Is Ears—George Martin

Celtic Blessings—Beth Richardson

Jack's Book of Blessings—Beth Richardson

Holy Envy—Barbara Brown Taylor

The Cake and the Rain—Jimmy Webb

My usual practice is to read between twelve and fifteen books each year. That's about all I can manage along with newspapers, magazines, biblical commentaries and Bible study preparation materials that cross my path. I was hopeful that I would read more during the weeks of lockdown, but my COVID bookshelf seems about average for me. I enjoyed each of the books on my list, but a few of them are standouts for me.

After watching the NBC drama series *Council of Dads*, which debuted on March 24, 2020, and had a ten episode run, I bought Bruce Feiler's book *The Council of Dads*, on which the series was based. The series was faithful to the book, and both had an easy to digest, heartfelt storyline.

I have a fondness for biographies, and after reading the John Lennon and Fleetwood Mac biographies unearthed in Steve's apartment, I discovered Jimmy Webb's *The Cake and the Rain*. The songwriter's autobiography chronicles his career from his days as a Colton, California, high school student to his amazing success penning hit songs for dozens of artists.

In the late spring I became aware of James Taylor's memoir *Break Shot: My First 21 Years*. Audible offered the book, narrated by Taylor himself, and I signed on to listen. This led to the discovery of two more celebrity biographies, *Here Comes the Sun: the Spiritual and Musical Journey of George Harrison* by Joshua M. Greene, and *Lightfoot* by Nicholas Jennings. These are some of my songwriting heroes, and I found their stories compelling. In the case of the Harrison biography, the author's approach to the "Quiet Beatle's" life through his spiritual development was intriguing. Although I don't share Harrison's enthusiasm for, or devotion to, Hinduism, it was rather fascinating to see how his faith influenced his songwriting, friendships, and associations.

The volume profiling Gordon Lightfoot fleshed out for me the background story of one of my all-time favorite singer/songwriters. Like the Harrison book, I first heard *Lightfoot*, liked it so much I bought it, and then read it. While I knew some of the facts in the book and had attended some of the performances referenced in the work, I appreciated learning more details of Gordon Lightfoot's life and career. Celebrity biographies of musicians often reveal what inspired a song, and I like learning those backstories. It also humanizes the star and encourages my own songwriting.

Robin DiAngelo's sociological study, *White Fragility: Why It's So Hard for White People to Talk About Racism* had been on my radar for a while. When I found it on Audible, I gave it my attention. I am a firm believer that racism is America's unfinished agenda. DiAngelo presents a reasonable argument for the phenomenon of white privilege and the difficulty our nation has with race relations. Having heard it, this was another volume that I sought to read.

Holy Envy, Barbara Brown Taylor's 2019 book, rounds out my COVID bookshelf. She is a delightful author with keen insight on religious thinking and influence in our culture. Her forthright writing style, illustrative anecdotes, and sense of humor come across in charming ways. It had been a couple of years since I had read one of her works, and I ordered *Holy Envy* as soon as I learned about it. Her subtitle reveals the nature of the book: *Finding God in the Faith of Others*. Her approach to various religious traditions draws out an understanding and appreciation of their value in the lives of other people. She contrasts her own life as a Christian clergywoman and reveals her envy of those sacred traditions—a very clever way to discuss the subject.

Our collective COVID isolation did not keep me from buying new reading material, and it gave me ample time for my pleasure reading. Like all good books, my COVID collection took me to faraway places, most notably England and Israel. These books introduced me to intriguing characters, particularly background figures who drifted in and out of the lives of celebrities. This reading list taught me new things about my world, especially the beliefs and practices of other religions. Each author entertained me well as the lockdown time was passing. It's a cliché to say that reading is a form of escape, but when books are informative and well-written, they also can be grounding and life-changing.

Overall, the lockdown experience was not particularly restrictive for me. Sure, there were things that I couldn't do, like eat in a restaurant. It was not possible to go to familiar places or meet up with friends. I adapted to virtual interactions with relative ease. When I think of those months of social isolation, I have positive memories of self-directed activities. I put those hours to good use, that I redeemed the time I was given. Was it easy? Not necessarily, but neither did I find it to be oppressive. Because of my tendency to keep myself occupied, I found enough projects to sustain my interest.

3

Making Pandemic Adjustments

IN A VERY SHORT time the public health crisis of this pandemic developed into an economic shock as well. Americans judge how strong their bank account is and see it as a measure of their prosperity. If the economy is struggling, we vote with our pocketbooks and elect leaders we hope will get us back on track. In this pandemic, as the economy began to teeter, many (if not most) business owners saw their bottom line dropping. The pandemic shuttered many restaurants, companies, childcare centers and other businesses. If the public can't get out to support your establishment, you won't have customers and you won't make money. This basic economic lesson played itself out in 2020.

Various closures altered how we conducted our daily business. People were laid off or jobs evaporated, especially among low-wage hourly restaurant employees. Many of those jobs had been occupied by minorities, so that segment of our population was hit especially hard. Schools and universities shut down, leaving students and employees up in the air. Theaters, stores, entertainment and sports venues closed, leading to more job losses. Some of the small business ventures shuttered for good when they could not sustain the losses. Life as we knew it was changing.

Those who could began to work from home, tele-commuting or tele-conferencing to be in touch with co-workers, doing research online, or directing employees who were also working remotely. Some discovered their productivity increased in the relative quiet and comfort of their personal space. Others encountered the challenge of sharing bandwidth with spouses also working from home, or children doing schoolwork. For each plus there seemed to be a minus; for the additional family togetherness there was the attention that family members demand. The stresses of working from home were compounded in homes where there are special needs or where caregiving duties had to be taken into consideration.

> **COVID TRACKING—June 2020**
> **Cases: 1,734,040 / Deaths: 104,900**

Our California-Pacific Annual Conference cancelled its traditional in-person gathering and met virtually in June 2020. (I missed the 2019 conference because I had knee replacement surgery.) Our Zoom Annual Conference meant that we were not on the campus of the University of Redlands for the first time in more than sixty years. I duly registered and learned how we would hear reports, ask questions, take votes, and celebrate the various ministries of our conference remotely. It was certainly cheaper and less physically demanding to hold the meeting electronically. What was missing was the deep in-person fellowship. (The event was to be held via Zoom for a second year in 2021.)

Since my 2013 retirement, I have not had to attend Annual Conference, although the input of retirees is welcomed. There are elements of our annual gathering that seem like a waste of time and energy. Unless one has a vested interest in a bit of legislation or a responsibility to fulfill, Annual Conference can feel like an exercise in futility.

On the upside, time to visit with colleagues and friends I rarely see is always the greatest joy of the event. It's fun to catch up on their lives, families, and careers. Sometimes I reunite with former parishioners and learn what's new in an earlier church appointment. Sometimes I learn of someone's struggles or a life-altering medical issue. I might hear of births, marriages, and life-changing decisions.

A virtual Annual Conference removes most of the personal contact, and much more official business gets accomplished. Each session serves to diminish my interest in the entire process. That attitude is probably a product of my age, my forty-year career, or both. While I do care about the church, I have less stake in its practical matters.

In addition to dealing with COVID our nation was in the midst of a contentious presidential election year. The incumbent Republican was deceiving the public about the pandemic. On February 7, he said the virus would "weaken by April with the warmer weather" and three weeks later said, "it will disappear."[1]

By April, he wondered aloud whether the injection of bleach into the human body could fight COVID. In a Bob Woodward interview, conducted on February 7 and released on September 10, 2020, President Donald Trump admitted he had intentionally withheld information that would have helped our nation get ahead of this public health crisis. "I wanted to play it down . . . because I don't want to create a panic."[2] Even in the summer he claimed the virus was "going to fade away" (June 17) and that his administration was "getting the pandemic under control" (July 2).

Meanwhile, the number of Democratic challengers diminished through the primary race, and one person became the de facto nominee. Joe Biden also addressed the pandemic, in a speech in Wilmington, Delaware, on March 12, 2020. With his characteristic compassion and empathy he noted how affected families "have suffered a loss, first responders and healthcare providers are putting themselves on the line . . . making sacrifices to protect us."

Mr. Biden also said that "public fears are being compounded by a pervasive lack of trust in this president. Our government's ability to respond effectively has been undermined by hollowing out our agencies and disparagement of science . . ." He called for widespread, free COVID testing, a surge in our capacity to both prevent and treat the coronavirus, and an acceleration of the development of a vaccine.[3] These were hopeful words for me.

Following the May 25 murder of George Floyd beneath the knees of Minneapolis police officer Derek Chauvin, the nation erupted with demonstrations of Black Lives Matter and Defund the Police. On June 1, the President misused police officers in riot gear to clear his path from the White House through Lafayette Square to St. John's Episcopal Church for a spurious photo op of him holding a Bible. In my view, this offensive display served no purpose except perhaps in the warped thinking of this apparent narcissist. His silent posturing only communicated his seeming lack of understanding and questionable faith.

---

1. "U.S. intelligence reports from January," *Washington Post*, March 20, 2020; "All The Times Trump Compared Covid-19 to the Flu," *Forbes*, September 10, 2020.

2. NPR, June 2, 2021.

3. "Former Vice President Joe Biden addresses," Youtube video.

Floyd's murder sparked demonstrations in many cities, most notably in Portland, Oregon, where a hundred days of protest began on May 28. The majority of the demonstrations began peacefully. However, some opportunists regrettably used these public protests as a cover for their unacceptable vandalism and looting. Whenever I see this happening, I wonder what value such destructive activity accomplishes. In Portland's case, these marches led to heated confrontations with law enforcement and counterprotesters. In my opinion, the excessive response from the police, including the use of tear gas and other weapons, exacerbated the peaceful objections of the public. In July, the federal government deployed its law enforcement officers to protect government property, adding pressure to the situation.

I saw all of this as a toxic soup of frustration, confusion, and anger developing. The degree of misinformation, disappointment, and bogus conspiracy theories led many to question the truth, or to wonder about the source of the truth they were hearing. In many ways, people were ignoring common sense, and little was being done to foster action for the common good. The political divide in our country grew more evident.

Local Adjustments

Closer to home, the Redlands Bowl—which "holds the distinction of being America's longest continuously running summer music festival where no admission is charged"[4]—cancelled their season of under-the-stars entertainment, interrupting a ninety-six-year tradition of summer programming. Civic clubs stopped their meeting schedules or adopted an online presence. Public libraries closed their doors and found new ways for the public to access their resources. Some companies developed a reservation system to maintain their business while limiting their client numbers.

Most elective surgeries were either cancelled or rescheduled. Physical therapy centers closed or operated with greatly reduced staff. Appointments with doctors were scratched or switched to telemedicine formats. I found it quite amusing when my podiatrist teleconferenced with me but couldn't physically care for my feet.

> **COVID TRACKING—July 2020**
> **Cases: 2,573,393 / Deaths: 128,182**

4. redlandsbowl.org

Many weddings planned for 2020 were postponed as travel restrictions took hold. Some weddings became elopements, or the events reworked as more intimate affairs. Likewise, schools and universities cancelled graduation ceremonies or adapted them as drive-by or virtual events. The longer the pandemic continued, the more some work-around strategies were implemented, reimagined with health and safety in mind along with the love and joy of such special occasions.

One of the saddest adjustments was the near elimination of funerals and memorial services. With the shocking number of deaths, there were multiple families who could not say a formal farewell to a loved one. Our funerary rites are usually public occasions to remember and honor a deceased family member. Such a service allows for closure or an acceptance of the death and provides a sad but loving tribute as we say goodbye.

From personal and pastoral experience, I know what a painful time the death of a loved one can be. Expected or not, a death can derail a survivor's life, and the losses multiply when there are tragic circumstances. I have often counseled with families about how to honor a life and how our faith celebrates the promises of eternal life. We've chosen Scriptures that speak to us and hymns that comfort us in the time of loss. Our choices also affirm God's ongoing love for us, bringing comfort and hope to families in grief.

While I did not lose a family member to COVID-19, several deaths touched our Redlands First UMC family in 2020 (not all of them COVID related). I did attend the viewing of a childhood friend's mother and was called upon to officiate one graveside service. In both cases, the coronavirus protocols were clear and observed. At other times I felt sad at not being able to attend one of the few services that were scheduled. Even more, my pastor's heart was heavy when families had to delay or not hold funerals or memorial services. The inability of families to have the support and comfort of public memorial services seems like a violation of a basic human need for ritual closure.

COVID robbed many people of this important ritual farewell, but a few alternatives developed. Certain services became graveside-only events or smaller-sized gatherings with limited capacity. Other remembrances were put on hold for a later time. So many heartbreaking losses and so much deferred grief means we all need to exhibit a good measure of compassion.

The impositions of this public health crisis did not seem to bother me or alter my daily routine. Even as a retired person there is always a reason to get out of bed, always a project underway or needing completion, always a task to be done or an errand to run. I am fortunate that I am rarely caught by a lack of interests to pursue. Each day has an element of appeal, maybe even a bit of adventure, though many days simply pass by quietly. I am intentional about taking breaks from whatever is holding my attention, and I give myself a change of venue for a while—a walk outside, something to dabble with—just stretching my legs is a welcome change of pace. When Sue is at home I can contribute to her projects, and when she is away, I have interests of my own to chase.

Each day can be measured by clocks and calendars, but the rhythm of light and dark has a more poetic effect on me. In the ebb and flow of time, I can negotiate the day and move forward without boredom. Like everyone, I have moments when my energy or focus lapses and I stare off into space. But before long a thought crosses my mind and I'm back to the project at hand or perhaps a new one. Life is too short and full of engaging things that there is no room for inactivity. Maybe that is a COVID lesson.

Irrespective of the coronavirus pandemic, there is so much of life that we leave unexplored. It intrigues me that there are languages I could learn, places I could visit, topics I could examine if only I applied myself. Even without a lot of money to invest, an intriguing subject can capture my attention for months. There is no time to be bored when I open myself to a new book or a conversation with someone whose interests, education and life experiences are different from my own. It doesn't take a public health crisis to spur my energies in the direction of something exciting and novel. And, as I was soon to discover, there was a favorite past activity that I would reclaim while restricted to my home.

> **COVID TRACKING—August 2020**
> **Cases: 4,456,389 / Deaths: 156,284**

In August, the California Department of Public Health (CDPH) introduced a four-tier risk-level tracking system for assessing the COVID threat in our state.[5] It was billed as a "Blueprint for a Safe Economy." It was used to help placate businesses and the general public who had spent five months under coronavirus restrictions. Every county in the state was assigned a level of risk that could be tightened or relaxed depending on two factors: coronavirus case numbers and positive testing numbers. As these numbers fluctuated, a county could move from a more restrictive tier to a

---

5. cdph.ca.gov/blueprint.

more relaxed tier but had to remain in its current tier for a minimum of three weeks before moving.

The color-coded risk-assessment system, which would be in place until June 15, 2021, provided a guideline for when businesses could operate or social activities could resume. The purple level was the most restrictive, the red level allowed for limited capacity in businesses; the orange level meant a greater capacity and yellow was the least restrictive. Since I didn't run a business, the system didn't mean that much to me. Mostly it restricted my access to stores or restaurants I frequent. It was frustrating not being able to enjoy lunch sitting inside a favorite haunt, but I simply chose to eat more meals at home.

The summer inched forward and before long I was on to another project. One of the things I said I wanted to do in retirement was write books. The coronavirus had given me the gift of time, so I set to work. Having previously self-published three books of poetry I knew the steps to take and began organizing myself for the task. I decided to work with material I had at hand and put together a book of sermons. (I had a whole file drawer full of sermons—my version of the proverbial barrel.)

I selected some of my favorite sermons for the Lectionary cycle. The Revised Common Lectionary is a three-year cycle of Scripture readings appointed for worship each Sunday in the liturgical year. I had electronic copies but I also pulled out hard copies so I could re-read them for consideration. My original hope was to select a sermon for each Sunday in each of the three liturgical years. A volume of over one hundred and fifty sermons began to feel excessive, so I settled on ten sermons per year for a total of thirty sermons. As the project developed, I added one bonus sermon for each year.

When this book project was about seventy-five percent complete, I landed on the idea of making it a three-volume set, corresponding to Year A, Year B, and Year C of the Lectionary. This made it easier to carry the project through the various production stages with Kindle Direct Publishing—a part of the vast Amazon empire. Eventually, *The Sermon Book* series included three subtitles: "Sowing in Good Soil" (Year A) , "I Can't See What I Believe" (Year B), and "Keep Your Apron On" (Year C).

Revisiting my sermons reminded me of the people who first heard them and the places where they were preached. Each congregation has a different personality, and I thought about the situations that brought these sermons to the fore. For example, the sermon "The Power to Forgive"[6] was written for a sermon series in September 2001, when the events of 9/11 rattled our country. I didn't preach it until the tenth anniversary of that tragic day.

I also became aware of how my preaching practices have changed over the years. There was a time when I preached from an outline, relying on spontaneity and my quick wittedness (possible gifts of the Spirit). My illustrations were sparse, my preparation incomplete. Halfway through my career I changed to being a manuscript preacher with the result of a better balance of Scripture, illustrative material, and a more well thought out approach to my chosen theme. I also switched from book references to film and modern media images as relevant interpretive examples.

As I wrote in the introduction to the books, I also reviewed the practical steps I have taken in the sermon preparation process—reading the Scripture, discussing an interpretive approach with colleagues, examining my theological framework, considering the worship setting and season, and the actual writing of the message. Preaching is such an ephemeral art that I was glad to have manuscripts to work with in creating the sermon books.

Interesting memories flooded back as I read and edited the sermons I had chosen. I thought of the worship setting in each church, and the faces of certain parishioners came to mind. I wondered if I had been true to the Scripture text I was using, and if the illustrations I had chosen were still valid or had become dated. In some cases, I recalled the world situation beyond the church or what life experiences I had brought into the sermon. My Trinity Sunday sermon, "Will You Dance?" used a photograph I took in the Chapel of the Pittsburgh Airport, and I wondered if it was still there after all these years (it is.)[7] These reflections had an element of nostalgia but also a sense of pride and accomplishment that I had faithfully presented the Gospel to the best of my ability.

I asked two retired clergy colleagues who are still active members of my Lectionary Study Group to serve as proofreaders. When they agreed I emailed them copies of the manuscripts for their review. Each pored over the books and made fine editorial suggestions, highlighting corrections I could make (but not on the sermon content). I am grateful for their thoughtful comments, which improved each volume.

In my enthusiastic rush to get this project into print, I made some mistakes. Fortunately, I had the sense to order proof copies of each book

6. Crisp, *Sermon Book (Year A)*, 77.
7. Crisp, *Sermon Book (Year A)*, 115.

so I could give each one a fine-tooth comb job of proofreading. To my consternation, I found numerous errors in each volume which I had the opportunity to correct.

Reclaiming Watercolor Painting

One day an idea came to me; I have no idea where it originated. Maybe it was a lull in my daily routine or the routine itself, but I started to think about picking up my hobby of watercolor painting. This completely enjoyable pastime has been a creative outlet for me in the past, yet it had been a long time since I had picked up a brush. I wasn't even sure if my supply of paints was viable, if I had paper to paint on, or if my brushes had any life left in them.

For several days I turned this idea over in my mind. The pandemic had slowed the pace of my life, activities had been postponed or cancelled, and I had time on my hands for reclaiming this leisure pursuit. After looking around the house and yard for a suitable subject, I decided to focus on a set of windchimes hanging on our pergola. I put more thought into the perspective, shape, and color scheme before I brought out my painting supplies. I drew sketches, took measurements, and made up my mind to press ahead.

Honestly, I was a bit afraid to resume this hobby. Although I had taken both public and private lessons years earlier, I wondered if I had lost my skills or my patience. Could I recover the techniques I had learned? Would the blank canvas stymie my approach? I had nothing to lose, so I set aside the time and began. About thirty minutes in, I was thoroughly enjoying myself creating art.

Watercolor painting requires focused attention, and it is easy to let cares and worries fade away as you paint. There are also several decisions to make—shape, layout, shading, color blending, depth and brush strokes. I have often been overly generous with the pigment, leaving a lot of color on the paper. Many watercolors are in pale, pastel shades, and while I admire that subtlety, it has never been my strong suit. I've also had trouble narrowing my focus, so I incorporate way too many images in my paintings. Given how much I pondered my approach to this process, I was ultimately pleased with the result. The bold colors seemed exactly right for the subject; I am proud of my windchime painting.

Just like that, my enthusiasm for watercolors had been rekindled, and I had a new activity to pursue during the pandemic. In the days that followed, I reviewed my previous paintings, my classroom notes, and a watercolor basics book, reminding myself of what I had learned so long ago. I found a couple of drawings I had made ten years earlier and selected a "10-by-14" lighthouse scene that had intimidated me enough to be set aside. Now it was time to face it and have fun.

With the same sense of care that I brought to the windchime painting, I contemplated my approach to the lighthouse. In other words, I took my time and let it develop naturally during my painting session. Not everything was easy, but with careful work I completed the piece and was satisfied with my accomplishment.

A switch had been flipped. The world outside was troubled with coronavirus cases, but on my patio a sense of calm took me miles away from those problems. I began to schedule two or three days a week for painting and bought some new supplies to expand my tools, including more paper in a variety of sizes to try my hand at different methods.

On those hot summer nights when I could not sleep, I quietly watched YouTube videos to learn new skills and expose myself to a variety of subjects. I learned how to blend colors for sunsets and trees, and how to get a handle on shapes and perspectives. A technique I had not thought of was monochrome painting—using a single color in painting. I was pleased with the waterfall, landscape, and city skyline images I copied from those video tutorials. After ten years, the bug had bitten me again.

Through the summer and into the fall, I painted each week and finished multiple paintings, large and small. I tried to do some freehand work—painting, not drawing first—and did a few pieces from detailed sketches to get the layout right. I explored shadings and color blending with new paints and studied ways of depicting mood or the time of day or night.

My thirst for fresh ideas led me to abstract expressions and stream of consciousness art. This discovery kept me well occupied at home and away from any exposure to COVID. For six months I painted many pieces and kept learning fresh things to try, giving me a gratifying outlet all the way to my illness in December.

Some of my artistic endeavors were complete failures, a waste of time and paint. Trying to use shades of red to paint an hourglass, I used so much color that the page screamed "RED!" An attempt to paint a self-portrait from a photograph produced a grotesque result. Despite several attempts, I could not master the delicate appearance of flower petals. But more important than any success was the act of painting itself, bringing me a sense of serenity in a chaotic time.

Following the success of my first lighthouse painting, I sketched two more, including a nighttime image, and made one of them in portrait orientation rather than landscape. Both returned to me a sense of accomplishment. My other subjects included churches, farm implements, silhouettes, autumn scenes, a winter scene and numerous landscapes. My inspiration came from magazine photos, internet images, online tutorials, and my own imagination. I was also quite pleased with the way a painting of Japan's Mt. Fuji emerged.

Because I was not attending church, Sunday mornings became a prime time for painting. Wednesday and Friday mornings were also set aside for painting. There was a spiritual feel to the art and a sense of peace that graced those days. On Sundays I would also listen to the "Breakfast with the Beatles" radio program (on KLOS) while I painted, adding another level of enjoyment to my rediscovered hobby.

> ### COVID TRACKING—September 2020
> ### Cases: 5,936,572 / Deaths: 186,292

In retrospect, I find it ironic and amusing that my sermon book writing and my watercolor painting took place during the COVID summer. They each seem to be artistic endeavors using both left-brain and right-brain activities. Left-brain dominance deals with words and verbal activities as well as facts, data and logical thinking (sermon writing). In contrast, right-brain dominance favors images and visualization, feelings, the arts and imagination (painting). Perhaps I have a well-balanced left-brain/right-brain way of operating.

Both sermon writing and watercolor painting are creative pursuits, and each discipline brings a variety of elements together. These pursuits came together when I had the time to invest in them. Sermon writing has been a part of my professional life, and I enjoy the research that goes into sermon preparation. My amateur painting is a hobby for relaxation and my personal enjoyment. Both are a part of who I am. I take comfort in a Kurt Vonnegut quotation I recently learned: "Being good at things isn't the point of doing them."[8]

The heat of summer did not abate as the season turned to fall. Our weekly rhythm became routine. Sue's work with the RCRC and the Trunk Ministry was a fulfilling expression of her compassion and dedication to serving the needs of others. My virtual meetings and artistic pursuits were absorbing my time and energy. These things carried on like clockwork.

---

8. Vonnegut, Kurt Quotes, accessed August 13, 2021.

Our household chores were likewise predictable—grocery shopping, laundry, house cleaning, walking the dog—each task adding to our overall well-being. Sue tackles the lion's share of these things and keeps our lives running smoothly. My contributions are small by comparison, but I participate in maintaining our "domestic bliss."

During the lockdown we didn't experience much of a role reversal, although I was home a bit more than Sue was. In the beginning, Sue did the grocery shopping because of my health risks, but later I did more shopping and prepared more meals. I've been known to vacuum the house, although that is a chore neither of us likes. When the weather is nice, we take up projects in the yard. I admit that I am easily drawn to activities that match my self-interests or one of the outside concerns that holds my attention. When I become absorbed in those things, domesticity takes a back seat.

The OSL Retreat

One of my jobs in the Order of Saint Luke is to plan and organize our annual retreat. The 2020 retreat had been in the works for two years when we had to cancel our in-person plans in favor of a virtual retreat. We made a plan that allowed for everything we would have at a normal retreat—presentations, business, breakout groups (informal and formal), testimonials, worship and fellowship—all via Zoom. The only thing missing would be the warm face-to-face contact with our brothers and sisters.

We developed a three-day format with events spread throughout the day, letting people join in when their personal schedules or work responsibilities would allow. Many OSL members are pastors and could find some flexibility in their daily activities. Our guest speaker, the Rev. Beth Richardson, agreed to this change of plans and graciously adapted her presentations to fit our altered schedule. The Rev. Beth A. Richardson is a member of the Mountain Sky Conference of The United Methodist Church. She serves The Upper Room in Nashville, Tennessee, as Director of Prayer and Worship Life and Dean of The Upper Room Chapel. Beth's theme, "Celtic Spirituality, Pilgrimage and Blessings," grabbed the attention of our OSL membership.

Although several OSL members reported having a measure of "Zoom fatigue,"—while not a formal diagnosis, the term refers to the exhaustion one feels after a video call or conference, akin to burnout—we had more than sixty members online at each session of the retreat. Members joined from the Philippines to Ireland and all points across the United States. Our worship services maintained the usual high degree of integrity, and our business was conducted in a clear and efficient manner.

> **COVID TRACKING—October 2020**
> **Cases: 7,115,491 / Deaths: 208,2253**

Br. Brent Isernhagen contributed significantly to the retreat by serving as our virtual host, helping with the many technical facets of the enterprise, allowing the retreat to be successful. True, we were meeting online because of the pandemic, but we put that in the back of our minds as we celebrated our ability to hold our annual retreat!

Beth's presentations recalled the concept of "thin places" in Celtic spirituality. I've always liked that idea and have found the idea in other cultures as well, particularly among Native Hawaiians. As I understand it, thin places are where two worlds are loosely knitted together, where the spiritual distance between heaven and earth has narrowed. While thin places may not be perceived with the five senses, in thin places I have sensed in a stronger way the presence of God. For me, the virtual format did not hinder the feeling of our gathering as one of those thin places.

I was certainly proud of the work I did to make our retreat a success. Dozens of decisions adjusting to the virtual format and increased communications were essential to keep everyone apprised of what seemed like a moving target. The details needed to keep everyone connected were too numerous to calculate.

∞⌘∞

I mid-October, I received a phone call from the Council President of Trinity Lutheran Church in Hemet asking if I would consider becoming their interim pastor again. I had served in that role for six weeks in 2014 (January and February, the season of Epiphany), and again in 2019 (March to June, for the seasons of Lent and Easter). Hemet is about thirty miles from where I live, and it is an easy commute. I have enjoyed my association with that congregation, and they have appreciated my preaching each time I have served there.

Because of the forced inability to worship together, they were holding services via Zoom like many other churches. Anticipating a return to in-person worship, they were looking to me for pastoral leadership whenever that would be possible again. After a weekend of pondering and praying about it, and talking it over with Sue, I decided to accept their invitation. I arranged for a meeting to agree on the details and began planning to start on November 1 with an All Saints' Day observance.

Unfortunately, in-person worship had to be further delayed, so we developed a new plan for me to begin in December. Still unable to worship in person, my sermons for December would be pre-recorded and added to the continuing Zoom services. Other parts of the liturgy were conducted in the safety of our teleconferencing. It was a joy to return to Trinity Lutheran and to work again with such faithful people who love and respect each other, and who dearly love their traditions and one hundred and five-year legacy.

Our Garage Sale

In the heat of the Inland Empire summer, Sue and I dedicated ourselves to getting ready for a garage sale. It was a tiring task and we limited our work to the cooler morning hours or spent a few evenings with this big project. Over the span of several weeks, things were sorted, classified and stored as neatly as we could in order to leave the garage useful for other needs. Due to COVID, we had nowhere else we had to be, and with this stay-at-home venture we were not putting others at risk. The work reminded us of other yard sales or garage sales we've had when moving and "lightening our load" or when we helped our son Matt move.

> **COVID TRACKING—November 2020**
> **Cases: 8,952,086 / Deaths: 232,295**

Unsure if we could have a garage sale with lockdown restrictions, we delayed having one until we noticed others in the neighborhood holding theirs. Even in a pandemic, bargain hunters will seek out a good deal. Although we had listed more valuable things on Craigslist, we sold nothing in advance, leaving us with a driveway full of treasures for people to look over.

A garage sale is lot of demanding work, but this was a successful one, and we tidied up with an overall sense of satisfaction for having finished the job. Normally, I would not think of a garage sale as a pandemic activity but given the amount of time and effort that the enterprise required, it provided us with a focus beyond the daily barrage of COVID news.

Feeling Lucky and Grateful

Sue and I considered ourselves lucky as this pandemic became so prevalent. Being retired and having both pension and Social Security income made us feel blessed. We didn't lose a job, our income remained steady, and our needs were being met. The frequent news reports of those who lost a business or a livelihood, coupled with reports of long lines for food, broke our hearts.

Due to the loss of income, people could barely afford to pay rent, maintain their health insurance payments or feed their family, sometimes having to choose which bill they would pay if they had any income at all. The long lines for food distribution, in my opinion, were a shameful sign of America's inequalities. People who never needed to receive this help were grateful it was available. The sense of shame or embarrassment was evident on their faces. The real disgrace was how unprepared our government was for this health crisis and how little compassion our leaders expressed for people in need. While I was glad to see that many faith groups stepped up to help with food donations and distributions, it felt like a spiritual crisis as well when the need outpaced the ability to help. The question also came back to, "What can I do to help?" The answer was not far away.

Locally, the Redlands Charitable Resource Coalition (RCRC) took action to help anyone who needed food be supplied with simple meals. The RCRC is comprised of people from non-profit and faith-based organizations and concerned residents of Redlands, who have come together to spotlight the issue of homelessness and to find solutions to those issues.[9]

In simple ways we did what we could to help as the COVID restrictions got underway. Sue, with a little help from me, first assisted in the RCRC effort to address food insecurity by providing sack lunches intended to cover two meals. At first these meals were distributed through one of three food stations in the city. Popup tents served as shelters at each distribution site. This was a small gesture on our part, yet one that served so many needing to be fed.

This operation began in March of 2020 and continued seven days a week during April and May. On June 1, the RCRC enterprise was consolidated to one location outside the Family Services buildings. The Redlands community donated sack lunches and food supplies for this effort. The

---

9. rcrchelp.com.

Family Service Association of Redlands (FSA) is and has been dedicated to helping those in need in the community since its founding in 1898.[10]

Trunk Ministry

For more than ten years, First United Methodist Church has had Showers of Blessing, a shower ministry for the homeless. Each Saturday morning, the showers in the basement of the church were made available to those in need. Because of the rapidly spreading virus, the last day the showers were open was March 7, 2020. Showers of Blessing often had hygiene items and clothing at the ready if anyone needed these goods. Sue was a leading volunteer for this ministry.

One day, while observing the RCRC food station in the parking lot of our church, Sue helped provide a client with supplies from the shower ministry resources. From that day forward Sue has carried a variety of items in her car to meet a variety of requests. Everything had closed up. The showers were closed. The folks on the street couldn't get a Share Meal. (The Share Meal was a weekly dinner provided and served by a variety of churches in the community.) As Sue says, "These people need help. There it is." This was the spark, the divine inspiration to begin what became the Trunk Ministry Sue has operated all through the pandemic.

In the back of her car, Sue has carried shirts, pants, underwear, hygiene items, shoes and socks, blankets, tote bags and backpacks, along with sunglasses and sunscreen, coats and hats to serve the needs of people living on the street. Sue posted a sign in her car which reads:

Redlands First
United Methodist Church
TRUNK MINISTRY
Clothing and hygiene items
for those without a home

Most of the people served have deeply appreciated Sue's welcoming attitude. She knows the names of those she helps and recognizes them around town. They also recognize her as the "Trunk Lady." They know they are cared for individually without prejudice or judgment, regardless of their circumstances. The responses from the recipients of the Trunk Ministry provisions are overwhelmingly positive (all are direct quotes):

10. redlandsfamilyservice.org.

- The best ministry in Redlands. You tell your pastor that.

- Thank you for doing this.

- I don't know what I'd do without you.

Sue offers a lot of what she calls "Mom hugs." She is keenly sensitive to people who appear to be having a hard time or a bad day. And the threat of COVID-19 did not keep her from offering her compassionate embrace.

Our garage became a sorting and storage place for supplies that come to Sue for the Trunk Ministry, and donations came from multiple sources. Our church family and folks connected with them were most generous. A Girl Scout troop from the Upper Desert provided socks, underwear, and several boxes of cookies. Family members, volunteers with the RCRC, and various community members made substantial contributions, including financial gifts. Inappropriate or unusable items—evening gowns and bed skirts, really?—were donated elsewhere or tossed.

What Sue didn't receive in donations she bought at the local Dollar Tree store to supplement the products she had available for distribution. She used the monetary donations to buy new underwear and socks, two highly desired items. Sue kept her Trunk Ministry well-supplied in anticipation of need. If she could, she would also acquire specific items when asked.

Working with both the RCRC and the Trunk Ministry has reaffirmed much of what she already believed. "The homeless are wonderful people," she says, and "they treat me with great respect." Some of the people Sue has met have been homeless for twenty years, some are struggling with mental health issues, and some are temporarily in a difficult situation but working a job, or looking for work to get back on their feet.

It has been clear that even in a pandemic, people are generous. Sue has not experienced the pandemic as other people have. She has been more active than ever. Sue asserts that everyone can make a difference, anyone can do this, but as she says, "serving others brings me joy." Another truth has become evident. Sue said, "Without COVID, I would not have had this experience." I am deeply impressed with her commitment to this work and enormously proud to be her husband.

For the first nine months of dealing with COVID, I was merrily rolling along with life. Overall, my mood was upbeat and my activity level had been strong. I was feeling thankful for my health and strength, grateful that I was not putting myself at risk, and if I'm honest, probably holding a *laissez faire* attitude. COVID changed all of that and landed me on my butt!

4

Testing Positive

THE WATERCOLOR PAINTING AND sermon books were summer projects. By September, I picked up another idea and began to develop another book. Twenty years earlier, I created a list of hymn suggestions for use with the United Methodist Church's songbook *The Faith We Sing*, selecting recommendations based on the Revised Common Lectionary. The Order of Saint Luke had previously put portions of my work in issues of their periodical *Sacramental Life*, but the work was incomplete. While looking over various files related to this idea, I discovered how incomplete the project was. For a few weeks I reviewed my notes and files, then tackled the work in earnest.

By slightly adapting the format I had used for *Sacramental Life*, the project came together with surprising ease. When the manuscript was complete, I pitched the idea to the Order of Saint Luke to publish the book. After some market research and a back-and-forth debate with Br. Daniel Benedict, the Director of Acquisitions and Author Relations for OSL Publications, the Order agreed to publish the book, and we invited Br. Robert Schall to be the copy editor. The pandemic was becoming a productive season.

With the pandemic in full swing for some months now, I found myself wondering if I had done all the right things to avoid COVID-19, or if I simply hadn't encountered it yet. I felt no sense of paranoia, as if the virus was lying in wait for me, but I thought about how there must be diminishing odds. Whenever I heard about a death in my circle of acquaintances, the "how did they catch it" question ran through my mind. Philosophically, it didn't matter; the person was gone. But knowing the circumstances of the death increased my sense of caution.

If I were to catch COVID, would that mean a death sentence for me? Would my case be a mild one, as so many people had experienced, or would I wind up on a ventilator awaiting my fate? I believed that the longer the pandemic continued the more we would learn, and as we learned more about the disease would be able to resist its ravages. I didn't dwell on these questions, but they crossed my mind in the quieter moments of summer and fall.

Other things demanded my attention, and the new book was set aside for a time. The book was essentially finished in the fall, especially after some re-writes in the introduction. The manuscript sat in my computer through Thanksgiving and into early December. Then I got sick with COVID and the whole project faded into the deep background of my concerns. It was a sign of my recovery when I returned to the project in January and pushed to get the book into print. The Order published *The Faith We Sing and the Lectionary* in February of 2021, and I was the proud compiler of a book that I did not self-publish.

Who is to say how one contracts a pathogen like the novel coronavirus? More than once, people asked me, "Do you know how you got COVID?" I've thought about that myself and walked my way through several possibilities.

Nine months into a life of COVID restrictions, Americans were urged to avoid travel and large family gatherings over the four-day Thanksgiving weekend. Tired of living with the virus, many folks scaled down their plans but decided to gather with their loved ones despite that advice.

Sue and I were among those who debated seriously making a Thanksgiving trip, ultimately deciding to make the five-hour drive to her sister Alyce's home in Los Banos for the holiday. Traditions have a strong influence on our behavior, and it had become our practice to travel to Alyce's for Thanksgiving ever since her husband Bill died in 2013. Our established pattern has become customary and includes familiar activities both along the road and during our stay at Alyce's. In some years, the holiday trip is the only time we get to see her, although we are in frequent phone contact with her.

We felt safe and agreed that we would follow every COVID precaution as we traveled. Along the way, the rest stops were less populated, clean, and had the services we needed. People were masked and social distancing.

We really weighed the value of keeping our tradition and making the trip or following the guidance of the public health officials and staying home. We reasoned that we would be on our own in the car, avoid large gatherings all week long, and have a small group of four at the table for dinner. Yes, we were at some level of risk, but the pull of our Thanksgiving tradition and the desire to *go somewhere* after so long at home won us over.

Alyce's son, our nephew Michael, who had been tested for COVID, would also be joining us, and a four-person gathering did not seem too large. Once we were at Alyce's, we stayed close to home apart from going to the supermarket and Walmart for supplies. One additional outing took us to several other stores. Pandemic protocols were being followed everywhere we went.

Instead of going out for our Thanksgiving dinner, as had been our tradition, and to avoid the labor of making a festive meal ourselves at home, we ordered take-out from the Black Bear Diner, a favorite dining spot of ours in Los Banos. The diner took care to make the pick-up process as contactless as possible, with proper procedures at each point. With just four of us at the dinner table—Alyce, Michael, Sue and myself—the threat of catching the virus during our Thanksgiving visit seemed minimal.

Our return trip stops were made in the relative safety of well-sanitized, socially distanced, and uncrowded places. We eliminated one of our usual stops to further decrease our risk. In the two weeks that followed our brief journey—time in which the virus could incubate—none of the four of us developed any COVID symptoms. Ultimately, I did not consider the trip to be the source of my infection.

After our return, my time spent away from home was so minimal as to be insignificant. I made a trip to J.C. Penney's to pick up an online order, then I went to Bed, Bath & Beyond to shop for a Christmas present for Sue. Honestly, those are the only two places I went between Thanksgiving and the ensuing two weeks.

Who knows what vapor droplets I was exposed to as I walked around those two stores? What virus bit might have transferred from hand to door-knob to me? What person came within six feet of me as I was shopping? Who knows how I caught COVID-19? Due to the incubation period of the virus, it is entirely possible that I caught it on the Thanksgiving trip. I briefly thought about this while I was hospitalized but didn't have the energy to seriously ponder this unanswerable question. Ultimately, it doesn't matter how, and I don't really care to pinpoint it any further. What matters is that I did catch the virus and became sick as a result.

COVID TRACKING—December 2020
Cases: 13,234,551 / Deaths: 271,235

On Friday, December 11, I had a Zoom call with my college roommate Jerry McBride. We hadn't spoken for a few years but we were glad to have connected on video. In the early afternoon, when Sue came home from her volunteering with the homeless, she noticed that my eyes looked awfully red. I thought they had been rather watery earlier that morning, but I didn't think much about it at that point. After telling me what she was seeing, I called to get a same-day appointment with a doctor but had no success. The next logical step was to take myself to Kaiser's urgent care clinic in Redlands, unaware that it had closed down nine months earlier due to the pandemic. Out of options on a late Friday afternoon, and not wanting to make the eighteen-mile trip to Kaiser's Fontana facility, I went home hoping things would be better in the morning.

My eyes were not any better in the light of day, so I drove to the urgent care clinic in Fontana where the Physician's Assistant on duty saw me. He diagnosed an eye infection and prescribed eye-drop medication, and I was told to return on Monday if my eyes didn't improve. I learned a lot later that an eye infection was one of the earliest symptoms of the virus, discovered and reported by an ophthalmologist in China. It is not one of the more common symptoms, which is why it was easily misdiagnosed.

I was oblivious to any connection between an eye infection and CO-VID. Rather than feeling any anxiety, I was annoyed that I had to follow through with a medical problem over an unencumbered weekend. Even the COVID protocols at the hospital door that Saturday morning did not raise any alarm. They had been in place for several months and were an expected part of going to the urgent care clinic. The list of screening questions was familiar enough, and I was having none of the listed symptoms. That I might have COVID was far from my thoughts.

I administered the eye drops on Saturday and Sunday, but things did not improve. By Monday evening, I made another trip to urgent care. This time the COVID protocols at the door kept me from entering the clinic without an appointment, and I had not been tested so I did not know my COVID status. That ended up in a phone consultation with "Dr. T" while sitting in my car in Kaiser's parking garage. I calmly worked on a few crossword puzzles while I awaited Dr. T's phone call. I was sitting two hundred feet from the clinic door, but due to my eye infection symptom they wouldn't let me walk into the clinic, as part of their COVID precautions. The doctor ordered my COVID test for the following day. It would take place at my usual Kaiser clinic in Redlands, four miles from home.

Tuesday morning, after eating breakfast and walking the dog, I drove to the clinic for my COVID test. I got into the line of cars circling the facility and waited forty-five minutes for my turn. I don't know why it didn't cross my mind that I might be infected. Sitting there was simply an inconvenience, and I was resigned to following through, if only to rule out the disease.

When it was my turn, I pulled into a designated parking slot and called the number to advise those running the test site of my presence. A few minutes later, a Licensed Vocational Nurse in full PPE presented me with paperwork. Another phone call told them my paperwork was ready. I remember thinking, "Here we go. Brace yourself for this test. You can get through this, and it will all be behind you." At that moment, I expected that the test would be negative. The LVN described what she was going to do, told me to grasp the steering wheel, then did the deep swab of my nasal passages. Her advice was to blow my nose and drink some water, both of which I did. She also told me I would get my results in twenty-four to forty-eight hours.

I drove away wondering what the test results would be, hoping I would not test positive for the virus but knowing that was a possibility. There is always a curiosity about what my medical tests results will be. The rest of the day I bounced back and forth between what either result would mean. If the test was negative, I'd breathe a sigh of relief and continue with my plans. If the test was positive, I'd follow through with whatever it took to address the illness. I frequently checked my personalized health care web page and waited. I don't think I overtly prayed about it one way or the other. I believe whatever happens, God will be my companion through the experience, good or bad. I am fond of Psalm 23:4 which says, "Even though I walk *through* the darkest valley, I fear no evil; for *you are with me* . . ." (emphasis mine). Whatever happens, God is ever-present.

To keep my mind off waiting, I spent some time preparing a sermon that I expected to deliver soon. Just two weeks earlier I had started to work at Trinity Lutheran Church of Hemet as their part-time, long-term interim pastor. I made video recordings of two earlier sermons and intended to record a third one the following day, but that didn't happen.

On Wednesday morning, December 16, my COVID test came back positive. I called Dr. T to ask what I was to do next in light of this result. When she called back, she gave me instructions. I was to drink Gatorade, take Tylenol, and use my Albuterol inhaler. She advised me to go to the Kaiser facility in Fontana, and she ordered a chest x-ray. I was to get a Pulse Oximeter at the drive-up twenty-four-hour pharmacy or have someone check my oxygen saturation level and pulse rate. (I was to become quite familiar with this little device.) If my oxygen saturation rate was less than ninety-three, I was to go immediately to the emergency room. I drove myself to Fontana and found a parking spot on the first floor of the parking garage—a rare occurrence. Struggling as I walked toward the clinic door, I had to stop twice to catch my breath. That should have been a clue.

When I finally got to the clinic door, the COVID screeners naturally would not let me in because of my being out of breath. I said I was there for a chest x-ray, and they called to verify my statement. A genuinely nice young man, Joseph, whom I had spoken with briefly before driving to Fontana, came out to meet me and escort me to the radiology department. At that point I did not think I could walk to radiology—clue number two—and asked if he could get me a wheelchair.

Joseph disappeared and a few minutes later returned with a wheelchair, and he took me in for the x-ray. I barely had the strength to stand or hold my breath while the x-ray was taken—yet another clue. Joseph then wheeled me to a medical office where my oxygen saturation level could be measured. My O2 level was eighty-six (or eighty-three?), so I asked him to take me to the emergency room. On the way, I asked Joseph if this was his usual job. He said it wasn't, and I thanked him for going the extra mile to take care of me. The core saga of my COVID crucible began.

5

The Hospital Experience

UNTIL NOW, I HAVE been describing my experience in the first nine months of the coronavirus pandemic. As a friend said recently, "It was more of an annoyance than really impacting my life." Essentially, COVID-19 had been a frustrating collection of news reports, social restrictions, misinformation and political wrangling, statistics and patiently waiting out the virus' presence in our midst. I was surviving the pandemic with relative ease—free to pursue my own interests, financially secure, retired with few responsibilities. All of that changed in mid-December.

Several portions of my original hospital blog will be interspersed with my text, italicized for easy recognition. (The complete blog is found in Appendix One, p. 123.) Notes for these observations were written on paper towels and other scraps of paper that I could find near my hospital bed. I wrote these reflections as they occurred to me after the fact and not in chronological order. I have noted the dates and titles I gave to the blog entries. I have not edited what I have written except to explain an incomplete thought or clarify a comment. Those edits are contained in brackets.

December 16, 11:45 am

Still in a wheelchair, I was moved into the traditional emergency room waiting area. It was nearly empty, with only a few patients awaiting treatment. COVID cases were directed to an outdoor area, which in non-pandemic times is a parking lot with an adjacent sidewalk. Tables were set up as a reception area where a few initial screening questions were asked. Behind them, other screeners authenticated my status as a Kaiser patient. Here I learned that my wait had begun in earnest; they told me it may be as long as ten hours before I would see a doctor.

Blog entry #4—The War Zone
December 21, 2020

That's what they called it, emergency rooms dealing with COVID-19 cases like mine. There was a list of emergencies but not much room in the traditional sense. Outside of the ER, a series of popup tents were serving as the "rooms." As I checked in with the ER, it was an area set up for admitting patients where they were taking some information about your medical insurance. I was then set aside to wait for a triage nurse. Since I was in a wheelchair, I could roll from the sunny spot given me to a place in the shade of 8–10 popup tents.

Everywhere I looked, in that makeshift waiting room that was no room, all I could see was hurting people leaning against a loved one or slumped over in a chair, waiting to be seen and treated. It was a sunny but cool day, and people were wrapped in blankets, layered with clothing, or bundled up in heavy coats, if they were lucky. To my left, a "hallway" of 10' x 10' popup tents had been created, lined with chairs 6 to 8 feet apart, each occupied by a potential patient.

On my right, beyond the admitting tables, was another row of popups lined with patients in folding chairs. In the elbow of the "L" was an open-air triage area with four or five stations. The nurses were in perpetual motion, calling out names and reviewing each person's need. Here they asked a deeper set of screening questions for each assessment. I guessed that about eighty-five or ninety patients were waiting for someone to call our name and help us.

Several of the patients were elderly and had a family member or caregiver with them. As it was lunchtime, a few patients had a lunch that a helper went to get from a fast food place, a vending machine, or the hospital cafeteria. Those without companions went without any food or were too miserable to consider eating.

. . . I was wheeled to the nurse triage area and my vitals were taken. I was rolled a few feet back to wait for another 10 hours for the next thing to happen. I had arrived at 11:45 a.m.

Blog entry #4—The War Zone

Time crawled slowly as I sat in the wheelchair, my breathing becoming more labored. In those moments I wondered what was happening to me. I knew I had tested positive for COVID-19, but I had not yet connected that to my breathing difficulties. The questions started coming. What is going on with me? Why am I here? I came here to get an x-ray and go home. What have I done? Where have I been? When will I be seen and treated so I could go home? There were no ready answers.

Those first few hours in the War Zone were a mixture of curiosity and observation. While enduring my long wait, I was pondering my situation, but there wasn't a lot I could do about it. As time progressed, my easygoing nature—a patient being patient—kicked in and I began to study the scenario before my eyes.

Without intending to, I was memorizing the layout of the area and mentally kept busy monitoring the activities going on around me (see sketch of the War Zone, Appendix Two, p. 135). I took note of who was suffering, and who might be a relative or companion. I tried to distinguish the role of each staff member by watching what they did. As each patient's name was called, I wondered when I'd hear my name.

During my time in the War Room, I lifted silent prayers for the staff and the patients around me. It was like Paul's encouragement to "pray without ceasing" (1 Thess 5:17), my petitions rising nearly by habit after years of praying for others in the hospital. But the weaker I became the less focused my prayers were. Later, when attentive care was given to me, my praying faded.

I gave no thought to worrying about myself. Looking back, it may have been a heavy dose of denial, or it may have been my mind protecting me from becoming stressed about my circumstances. I remember feeling that I was in this large outdoor waiting room, and when it was my turn I'd be seen, treated and be on my way. This *was* the COVID case waiting room, and I had tested positive for the virus, but I must have been naïve about what I was facing. Although I was sitting in the War Zone, I had not crossed that bridge to thinking of myself as a COVID patient.

Once or twice over the next few hours, I called Sue on our pay-as-you-go cell phone. I had taken it with me as a last-minute suggestion from Sue. There was not a lot of charge left so the calls were short with few updates to offer. Whatever slim progress had been made as the time passed was all I had to report. I still had in mind that I would be seen and treated, then released to go home.

From my mobile perch, I watched as patients were moved about for whatever care they were to receive, but the number of patients did not seem to decrease. For every patient called for treatment, another poor soul entered the COVID waiting area. In addition to the sound of many conversations, the waiting area echoed with the moans and groans of the suffering. People cried out for help, and maybe someone would respond. There was the clatter of tables and chairs being moved to where they were needed. Occasionally, one of the medical staff had to do a little crowd control—barking orders in a stern, forceful way to bring a few impatient people back to a sense of calm. Watching all this activity unfold kept my thoughts on the human theatre before me rather than sinking into the quagmire of misery and uncertainty as the hours passed.

I watched as the afternoon descended, turning into night. Safety lights came on, streetlights came on, space heaters were ignited—none of which dispelled the gloom of despair on the people's faces.

Along about 8:00 pm, I was given an IV, and I asked for a blanket. A rough cotton stadium style blanket was provided. I was grateful for the protection as the cold and wind were increasing. The street noise from outside the hospital was also increasing as traffic came and went at the intersection of Valley Blvd. and Sierra Blvd.

As the evening wore on, the noise became distracting. You could hear the planes as they approached Ontario Airport. The buses came and went according to their schedule, their air brakes sounding as they stopped nearby. The Union Pacific trains passing a quarter mile away seemed to be just beyond the hospital wall. There was sound from the freeway, speeding cars and hundreds of 18-wheelers thundering by. What I presumed were hot rod cars were peeling away from the traffic light as though in a race—the drivers having invested money in their machines—but showing no concern for the patients. A lot of noise, amplified by the muted darkness inside the War Zone.

Blog entry #4—The War Zone

I did a lot of waiting that night, and there was more waiting to be done before the staff addressed my needs. People came and went, impatient with the time it takes to sort through so much human suffering. I couldn't help but overhear snippets of conversations, the welcome words of a patient being released, or the grumbling of those in misery. Every now and then I was able to catch a medical worker's ear and have a question answered. Aware that the COVID outbreak had strained medical personnel everywhere, I did my best to observe what I could and kept to myself.

I'd like to think I managed to be mindful of my needs, without demanding any special treatment. Usually I am able to logically address what's happening around me, but I could tell everything was not adding up right. Months of news reports had told how medical workers were stretched thin, especially during the spikes in cases. I could see around me how the nurses were continually on the move, responding to people's cries for help. I could hear the ambulances arrive with new patients and have nowhere to offload them. A level of empathy for others is part of my sense of self, but that night I could feel my emotional strength ebbing away, and my thoughts as well.

Blog Entry #1—Four Nurses
December 18, 2020

The front line medical workers in the coronavirus pandemic have been rightly hailed as heroes for the dedicated work they do in caring for COVID patients. I became one of those patients on December 16 and witnessed first-hand the knowledge, skills and compassionate care the nurses provided in a challenging environment. With a ratio of six to one, the nursing staff was stretched thin and had to deal with multiple questions and requests for help from their patients. Here is a brief sketch of four of those nurses.

Randi—At first she didn't tell me her name, and it took a while to determine that she was, in fact, an RN and just one of dozens helping with the massive triage happening around me. She was smart and sassy, both the good kind and the bad of sassy, so you wanted to stay on her good side. She was kind and would do anything for you. She could tease just enough to make you wonder, then pull you back to the truth of the matter before you were done. At what was supposed to be her personal rest time, she provided three or four of us patients with a hot meal—I suspect at her own cost—just before the end of her shift. She was gone with no way to express my gratitude for feeding me.

The next few hours are not clear in my mind. I know I needed to use the portable potty I had spied across the courtyard. It had been too long a time since I had relieved myself, so I was getting desperate. When I got his attention, a nurse named Aaron helped me out.

Aaron—A tall, self-contained man in his early 30's, I first met Aaron on my first night in the circle of hell known as the COVID waiting room. The "room" was a three-sided popup tent where all we did was wait. Aaron's task was to lead me to the bathroom, the first opportunity to do so in about ten hours. That meant maneuvering me and my wheelchair through a crowded seating area to a portable toilet. He was concerned about the appalling condition of the unit and called [Environmental Services] before I had completed my business. Despite the mess, it was the best I had felt since arriving at the ER. Aaron squired me back to my waiting position and I waited five more hours before there was another change.

Blog Entry #1—Four Nurses

Somewhere around 2:00 am, I was moved to the structure in the courtyard called the "Noodle." This structure was actually a large, soft-sided tent. Inside, there was room for ten beds, six of which were occupied including me. When I say bed, I mean gurney, but that was better than one of the lounge chair style "beds" that was the option. I knew I would be safe there and could try and get some sleep. It was cold inside, the lights on all the time with no chance of dimming, and a continuous flow of air circulated loudly. [In addition to the gurney, the other advantage to being in the Noodle was that I was given oxygen, with frequent tank changes as the oxygen was used up.]

Blog entry #4—The War Zone

I received oxygen through a mouth and nose mask via a high-flow nasal cannula. I did not know then, but I was suffering with acute hypoxemic respiratory failure. A couple of days later, Dr. Ian Casimiro reported to Sue that I was receiving a "fair amount of oxygen."[1] The dose of supplemental oxygen is usually 3 liters per min (L/min.) and I was currently receiving 15 L/min. The goal of oxygenation is for the patient to retain a self-sustained O_2 saturation range of 92 percent to 96 percent.[2] This is the stuff I learned long after becoming a patient.

1. Crisp, Sue, December 20, 2020.
2. National Institutes of Health, "Treatment Guidelines," December 12, 2020.

Vincent—Quietly working through the night, Vincent was unassuming of the burden he carried. For the six patients in his care, the most allowable, everyone got what they needed—vitals taken, medications given, labs, finger pricks [for blood sugar readings], shots—you name it, he seemed on top of the task. He responded when I answered one of his questions with a play on words, saying, "Ah, sense of humor intact." He gently shepherded us through the night when the change of shift released him to the morning.

Sue is the Facebook wizard in our house. She regularly reads the posts of her Facebook friends and enjoys a laugh or two. She also knows it as an effective form of communication. Naturally, Sue reached out to her Facebook network of family and friends. While I was waiting to be assessed in the War Zone, she posted a simple message: "Asking my family and friends to pray for my husband George. He has COVID and is not feeling great." In no time at all she had received seventy-three replies. The word about me spread far and wide.

In the middle of the night—I recall it being about 1:30 am Friday morning—I was informed that I would be getting my first dose of a drug called Remdesivir. Before that happened, Dr. Casimiro had briefly visited me in the Noodle. I don't know if he visited other patients, but he was at my bedside with some news. I had COVID pneumonia. My disease was no longer a vague diagnostic mystery. The doctor was concerned that I had used up three or four tanks of oxygen and my breathing was not improving. It was now time for the recommended treatment.

The puzzle pieces were falling into place. I had tested positive for COVID-19 on Tuesday. It had been hard to walk into the clinic for a chest x-ray Wednesday morning. My oxygen saturation had dropped to 83 percent and I was in the Noodle after going through COVID triage. I was sucking down oxygen as if it were water, and I was dying of thirst.

Somehow I had not put all of this together I experienced each part but had not grasped the big picture. I had COVID. This was something I had avoided for nine months. Other people were infected, thousands were hospitalized or dead. People in nursing homes had the highest risk; those who attended "superspreader" events came down with it. I did not realize this in the moment, but the evidence was obvious: I had become a statistic.

When I think about this now, I'm sure that I did not want to be a *death* statistic in this pandemic. Instead, I had become one more number among the thousands of people with this disease. With specific treatment for COVID, I could not avoid being part of the case tally, but if I had to be a statistic,

I wanted to be among those who recovered from this awful virus. What I had kept at arm's length was now an existential reality I could not deny.

Blog Entry #9—Medication
December 29, 2020

Early on in my hospitalization, I was given two medications meant to address the COVID-19 pneumonia ravaging my system. At the point they were first given to me, it was simply a matter of acceptance that I was receiving the meds. They were simply described to me as a steroid (Dexamethazone) and a drug developed for [treating] viral infections (Remdesivir). I subsequently learned that the steroid's purpose was to open the airways in my lungs while the Remdesivir was to counteract the COVID-19 virus specifically.

Grateful that a course of treatment was imminent, the news provided me with a good measure of relief. Without any knowledge of what this treatment would be like, I readily accepted the bagged medications hooked to a pole and fed intravenously, first the steroid and then the Remdesivir. The Noodle was still cold, and the medicine felt even colder as it entered my arm. I lay back intending to rest. But that didn't happen.

Even though I was aware of the room around me, I began to see bright white lights surround me. I knew I was lying in bed, but I was seeing myself in a lowered position, maybe two feet beneath me and off to the right. As I saw myself lying there, an extremely bright light enveloped me.

I had a clear sense of hallucinogenic effects for at least one of the drugs. (I was told it was not the Remdesivir but the steroid.) Each time I was to receive the drugs, I felt I had to brace myself for their effects.

At the onset of treatment, I saw flashes of bright white light, heard loud noises, and I would randomly shout out brief, clear sentences (in my mind) that came out as mumbled words.

Blog Entry #9—Medication

The IV drip had been in my arm for a little over an hour, long enough for the drug to empty out of the bag above my head. Exhaustion overtook me, and I slept for about three hours. I was awakened by someone changing the oxygen tank. I remained in bed, quietly resting but not asleep for the remainder of the night.

Around 6:30 am, I started hearing voices outside the Noodle. Then came the sound of saws buzzing their way through lumber. Hammers hitting nails and the whir of electric screwdrivers soon followed, along with the conversation of the hospital engineers working on the project. The patients in the Noodle began to stir, and the ambulatory ones went to investigate what was happening. The report came back that something was being built.

It turned out they were making a raised wooden walkway to ease the movement of patients in the courtyard serving as the large open-air CO-VID waiting area. They were still mid-construction when I was escorted to the portable potty again. Shortly after I returned to the Noodle, a nurse named Ben made his impressive entrance.

Ben—Ben announced himself with a booming voice and an apology: "My name is Ben, and I'm here to take care of you today, and I'm sorry for the condition I find you in. We're going to change that starting now." It was at once his self-proclaimed marching order and a sign of hope to each patient. Ben took charge, making a simple, quick org chart, checking everyone's vital statistics, talking to each patient, and even delivering us breakfast. Every spirit in the room brightened.

He steadily worked through every task, every wrong he felt needed to be made right. He did enlist the help of one additional RN, Marie, who came from a large OB/GYN clinic nearby. Her clinic's staff doctors had taken a vote and decided that half of them would help out in the hospital overrun with virus cases. She said she would be here through March. Marie followed Ben's well-thought out plan which really shook out the tablecloth and reset the table in an orderly manner, doing as he promised in his morning announcement.

While attending to my needs, I asked Ben where we got his training. Expecting the answer "the military," I was surprised to learn it was at Riverside Community Hospital. He expanded on that a bit, about how he got into emergency medicine through a series of better-paying jobs over time. He walked away at one time, working at a nearby Wendy's, but was hired by Kaiser in an on-the-spot-interview.

This exchange gave me the opportunity to tell him how much I appreciated his take-charge attitude carried out with compassion and reasonable empathy. It gave us hope and encouragement in a situation where "miserable" is the one thing you can speak about in the dire condition in which we found ourselves.

Blog Entry #1—Four Nurses

Somehow I missed the staff's shift change, so I never got the chance to say goodbye to Ben. He was simply gone.

The hours are long when you are too sick to get out of bed. This time was quite different from previous hospitalizations for surgery. With my knee replacement, I remember the encouragement to get out of bed and move. Now I did not have the breath support to walk very far. Like every patient, as the minutes become hours I was left to my own thoughts while I looked for ways to keep myself occupied. Often, poetic ideas form during long periods of thought. In my present situation, I began formulating what would become my first reflective notes on this experience. I didn't want to forget the names of the nurses I had encountered or the way they interacted with me. I asked for some paper but no one had the time to get any. The idea of using some paper towel came to me, and on my next visit to the facilities I brought back an extra length for this purpose. Since I usually carry a pen or two with me, I knew I had that need covered. I began writing the "Four Nurses" (Blog#1) from my bed in the Noodle.

Aaron returned the next night and was the charge nurse in the tent into which I had been moved for treatment. I had been moved to a gurney at 2:00 am, five hours after Aaron had helped me to the bathroom. It was a far site better, and I could stretch out and sleep a little. As Aaron's shift began, he welcomed me with a "Hi, buddy!" acknowledging our acquaintance of the previous night. Finding conditions greatly improved, he carried on with the task at hand caring for the patients. While not using such a precise method Ben had used, Aaron tended each patient with respect, focused medical care, and empathy, repeating each test, delivering every dose of medication, and serving each of us with medicines to give us strength. Daylight came and went, but I only left once, at night, to use the portable potty in the courtyard.

All of the medical servants do highly repetitive work with an ethic that is the content of their character. All are at war with a virus that leaves the patients they see coughing uncontrollably, feverish, in pain, depressed, and seeking some measure of relief. Who knows what satisfactions and benefits they receive for their difficult work—monetary, sure, caring for others, using their knowledge and expertise, supporting their family, helping our nation through its [worst] national health crisis in my lifetime. All of the above a scarce measure, I suppose. I only know how grateful I am that each one took care of me.

Blog Entry #1—Four Nurses

Throughout my time in the Noodle an oxygen tank was pouring 15 L/min. into my lungs. Someone on the staff would check the gauge to see how much oxygen remained and make sure that the face-mask was properly placed. The only time it was not in place was when I dozed off and it slipped out of position.

On my second night at Kaiser, I became aware that one reason I was having trouble sleeping was the absence of my C-PAP machine. For people like me with sleep apnea, a Continuous Positive Air Pressure machine steadily forces air into the lungs during sleep when otherwise breathing would stop. I asked Aaron if I could have the doctor order a C-PAP for me, and he said he would make a note of it for the doctor. A C-PAP machine never appeared throughout my hospital stay despite repeated requests.

Before I left the Noodle, I received a second Remdesivir treatment, again in the earliest hours of the day and about twenty-four hours after my first treatment. Knowing what had happened before, I was a bit anxious. I braced myself in anticipation of another round of the drug's effects. The chill of the medicine in my arm was back and the bright white lights returned but were less intense. Like the first time, the episode lasted a little more than an hour before I was disconnected.

The following morning, at about 2:30 am, I was tapped to move up. [Despite the oxygen mask, my oxygen saturation level dropped to 70%, far below the 93% that is standard.] The Noodle was still considered an ER room, but with a low O2 saturation level, I was taken inside the [hospital] building and placed in an ER bay. Nothing was done to me / for me there, other than to put me on a wall unit oxygen port and remove the tank, but I was placed on a nicer gurney. Still, the ER staff seemed indifferent to my presence. After just two hours there, I was moved to my actual hospital room. Here I have been cared for well and by kind, compassionate people, the dark brooding despair of the War Zone behind me.

Blog entry #4—The War Zone

When I had arrived in the War Zone at mid-day, it was sunny and breezy with chilly air. People were moving around to claim a spot in the shade or out of the wind (as I did) while the hospital staff did their best to keep up with the demand of the patient load. That bright atmosphere belied the misery of each patient who checked in and began to await their turn for treatment. As day became evening, the despair seemed to multiply, and patience diminished with the light. With nightfall, the suffering continued but the weariness of the day quieted the crowd.

At last, after more than fifty hours in the Noodle, I was wheeled into the hospital building. What I remember of the emergency room comes from the brief two hours I spent there. I was put into a room with a sliding glass door and hooked up to an oxygen supply. It was now early Saturday morning, December 19. I could see the nurses as they received the report on my condition and began making decisions on my care.

A male nurse came into the room to check on me but left in less than a minute. Several people passed my room or stopped to converse at the nurse's station within my sight. A few cast glances in my direction but did not come in. Later, a female nurse came in to check on my status and quickly left for other concerns. My COVID contagion was becoming even clearer.

I was pretty weak, and my mind was too cloudy to have asked either nurse what was going to happen with me. Although I had questions, I couldn't seem to ask them, either because I was sleep deprived, or because the disease had fogged up my brain. Everyone who came near me put on a new gown, gloves, hair coverings, medical grade face masks, and face shields—the ubiquitous PPE. The pace outside my room increased to a flurry of activity, and it wasn't long before I learned I was on my way to the hospital room that would be my home for the next ten days.

As I have done in other hospital settings, I studied the route they were using to transport me. Having walked the halls of many hospitals, I like to keep track of the pathways used to negotiate the labyrinth of departments, if only to find my way out again. It helps me to have some sense of the familiar as I am moving from place to place. That becomes even more important when I am the patient being moved. In my poor condition, I kept losing track of the hallways, the left and right turns we were taking, and which floor button on the elevator had been pushed. Hospital personnel know the shortest or most efficient route to use when moving patients around.

As efficiently as possible, I was transferred to a bed in room 708-B. I was the second patient in the room, and my bed was near the window. The shade was drawn but I could see the light of the morning before the sunrise as I was shifted into the bed. On the surface, it looked like a standard hospital bed, and I didn't notice it at first, but the mattress was designed and manufactured with ridges, dips and rises to keep the patient from lying flat and from lying too long in one position.

Grateful for the bed, I happily took to it and made it my own. The bed itself could be adjusted to raise my head or my feet, and that became an important feature. At that early stage, however, I had not discovered any of these things about the bed I would occupy for the next ten days.

Before long, a nurse arrived to check my vital signs and help me settle into my new situation. Throughout the transitions from the Noodle to the ER to the hospital room, I had been connected to an oxygen supply. I later learned that I was still receiving 15 L/min. of oxygen.

Besides the blood pressure and temperature checks, the LVNs and nurses did blood sugar finger-stick tests. [LVNs refers to Licensed Vocational Nurses and I use nurses to refer to Registered Nurses.] All COVID patients received blood sugar testing, not just those with diabetes or who were pre-diabetic. A lab worker came in about 6:30 am every day to draw blood for the day's analysis. There were fifteen- or twenty-minute gaps between these events so there was just enough time to get comfortably situated before I was interrupted again. These encounters did not do much to encourage rest. It was a relief when breakfast arrived, and I treasured the food I received. Having had little sleep for a couple of days, I was lucky to get a two-hour nap after breakfast.

I don't know if my roommate was welcoming of my arrival or simply tolerant of another patient with COVID. He had little choice in the matter, and besides, he was a COVID patient too. His name was Alfredo, a well-groomed, handsome man with a neatly-trimmed moustache. He was in his mid-seventies and stood about five foot six. Alfredo was near the end of his hospital stay, and after two days, he was discharged.

During our first conversation, Alfredo encouraged me to use the sanitizing wipes the staff had given me. Someone had impressed upon him the importance of using them before a meal, after using the bathroom, or any other time I wanted to sanitize my hands. Without telling him that I knew about using the Sani-Hands, I thanked him for his advice and promised to use them.

The next few hours passed with only brief interruptions. At the time of the shift change, the incoming nurses recorded my vital signs. Someone did an assessment of my regular medications to set up a pharmaceutical regimen for my hospital stay. If my blood sugars were out of the expected range, I would receive an injection of insulin, in place of the metformin which is part of my usual medication regimen. Everyone who came into the room for me made sure my oxygen flow was being maintained. Although I was still pretty weak, I tried to learn each person's name and make pleasant small talk with them.

I was given an extra-long amount of O2 tubing so I could reach the bathroom on my own. I was also attached to a telemetric monitoring system. Physically connected to me through several electrode leads, the device tracked my heartbeat and respiration, relaying this information to the nurses' station. The wires and tubing always seemed to get tangled up until I figured how to negotiate my movements while hooked up to machines. That first morning in the room I was getting the lay of the land and learning about my limitations. When I let myself relax, I drifted off to sleep for short periods of time.

Lunch was a welcome diversion, and the rest which followed helped restore some sense of normalcy to my predicament. An unexpected visit from Dr. Casimiro brought a bit more news of my condition. He was going to order a CT scan to determine if there was a blood clot in my lungs. My oxygen saturation was wavering in the 86 percent to 96 percent range, but that was with the assistance of the 15 L/min. of supplemental oxygen.

Also on that first day, I learned that I could use the telephone in the room to call home. I reached out to Sue to tell her where I was and what I had experienced since our last conversation. I told Sue that I was planning to sit up in bed and do some writing if I could summon the energy. It was now the third day since I had left home. If I had to be in the hospital, I was grateful to be in a comfy room.

Every two or three days Sue posted Facebook updates. Sometime after I spoke with her by phone on December 18, she posted this message: "Please continue to hold George in prayer. He is in Kaiser Hospital with double pneumonia." Former coworkers and distant connections got in touch to offer their support to her.

While I was getting settled into Room 708-B, our son Matt became ill with COVID-19. His case began with a high fever, and he soon developed diarrhea and a great deal of fatigue. These were the more expected symptoms of the disease so Matt arranged through the VA Hospital to be tested on December 20. No surprise, his test came back positive the following day. He quarantined himself for the next ten or more days as his body fought off the virus. Unfortunately, Matt was probably exposed to COVID by being around me, but fortunately his case was milder than mine was turning out to be.

On December 20 , Sue posted, "Update on George—He said he feels a little stronger. Doctor said he needs to get oxygen use lower in order to come home." Many people replied to Sue saying they were praying for me.

While the nurses' names were fresh in my mind, I had written the first of my blogs in the Noodle so I would not forget to celebrate the nurses who cared for me. In the quiet moments of that first afternoon in the hospital I wrote another entry, reflecting on myself and the COVID swimming in my system. I had some conflicting ideas about what I was going through which came out in these thoughts.

Blog Entry #2—A Lonely Disease
December 19, 2020

COVID-19 is a very lonely disease. It is happening to you. You are experiencing the loss of control in your lungs. You are making a cough you've never felt or heard before. You are the one who has lost the ability to have a normal night's sleep.

COVID-19 is not a very lonely disease. You come to the hospital for help because you know they are helping people there. You've come to seek answers, search the face of these helpers for release from your pain and frustration. You know you need help because that is what they do with suffering people like you.

COVID-19 is a very lonely disease. As you wait, in some cases 8, 10, 12 hours or more, you do a lot of thinking. How did I get here? You consider every option at the length your fevered brain will let you. You ponder every nuance of your life. As your eyes flash across the room at others as sick or worse than you, you see the misery you're in. Your eyes take in the helpers and you pray they stay strong—for you, for others, for what's next.

COVID-9 is not a very lonely disease. If you have one person, a family, friends who care for you, you are not alone. The wider your circle of friends, there is someone concerned, worrying, imagining what you are going through. You are now the person who has COVID-19, and [your experience] is one step closer to [them].

Sundays are relatively quiet in the hospital, at least for the patients. COVID restrictions prohibited any visits from family, friends, and even pastors. Already a sense of boredom was setting in, and I needed some clean underwear. I asked Sue to come to the hospital with supplies but noted that she couldn't bring them to my room. I directed her to leave the items at the security station near the hospital door. Sue brought a phone charger, two pair of underwear, and a newspaper, leaving them with my name on the bag with the security guards. These things were delivered to my room later in the day, and I relished the clean clothes and devoured the newspaper!

Blog Entry #3—You're the Patient
December 20, 2020

Of course you are, that's why you're here in the hospital and at every moment you are aware that you are the patient. Whether recovering from disease, surgery or injury (there are many reasons to be hospitalized), your job is to be the patient. How could you be otherwise? You don't feel up to anything else. Your energy level is low or non-existent, your breathing is poor or erratic, your thought processes have been scrambled. You are reduced to being a human being and you're grateful for all of the things you can do—feed yourself, get to the bathroom (hopefully on time), lie down, cover yourself, rise up after some much needed rest. You can answer questions, make basic requests, and there are brighter moments when your sense of humor kicks in and lightens the mood. None of this changes the fact that you are the patient.

COVID-19 patients have a fair amount of waiting ahead of them. You wait for medicine to come in little paper cups or to be injected into your body—sometimes directly, sometimes via an IV line stuck in your arm unceremoniously early on in your patienthood. You also wait, somewhat less eagerly, for the phlebotomist to draw your blood at an ungodly hour for the day's baseline labs. In an equal but opposite measure of eagerness, you wait [for] your meals. Sometimes you have the opportunity to pre-order your meal choice and wait to see if it comes as requested. With COVID-19, there is no rehabilitation to go to, no physical therapist who comes to you, but you wait in the hope of someone to give you an update on your health. That's why you've had all those tests. The update you're waiting for is, of course, good news of progress toward recovery and health.

The someone you want to hear from most is your doctor. His/her visit is normally once a day and very brief. You're given an update based on the data in your medical chart, not the doctor's personal observations. If you have had the strength and clarity of mind you may have formulated some questions for the doctor and you waited with concern to ask, hoping you don't leave something out of the question and answer session with your doctor and he/she actually listens enough to fully answer you. If something is not quite right, the specter of a new test is on the horizon to rule out an issue or clear a suspicion in the doctor's mind. Of course, you want this too, and a bit of waiting for the test and its results are set in motion.

Ultimately, you are waiting for the joyous news that you can go home, but you still might have to wait before that happens. Naturally, you want to be strong enough to go home, feel like going home; you want the going home to mean you're well enough to go home. You're eager to put this behind you, stop being the patient, but apprehensive about all you know is at home. Yes, you want to be better and anticipate you shall be, but how soon? When will you be 100%? When will you resume normal functions and actions? More things for which you wait.

I received the third Remdesivir/Dexamethasone treatment overnight. Again, I experienced the previous effects of the drugs—the cold medication, a vision of bright lights, the sight of my lowered body, the sound of indistinguishable words shouted at random times. Although I had braced myself in anticipation, actually holding on to the rails of the bed, the effects were as memorable as they had been before though with each treatment they seemed less intense and lasted a briefer time.

After the medication was administered, I tried to get some sleep. However, the lights in the room had been left on and the curtain between us patients had not been fully drawn closed, which would have blocked some of that light. I tried a variety of positions to turn my face away from the light, but never found a comfortable spot to bring about any sleep. That first weekend in the hospital was quite unforgettable and active for someone who didn't have a lot of strength and couldn't catch his breath.

The next day, with my fourth Remdesivir treatment, again within the first two hours after midnight, a new vision appeared. In this dream-like state, I began to see an image of a fat bird, which I took to be a duck, in the center of a wooden plaque, a straight line dividing the rectangle in two. A baseball hat with a long bill seemed to rest on the bird's head, but as the bird moved it became the bird's exceptionally long, pointed beak.

Many shades of brown drew my interest. The upper half of the plaque was golden brown, the color of light brown sugar. The bird's hat/beak was almost tan. The bottom half of the plaque was dark brown and the shadowy edges of the plaque were an even darker, mahogany brown. Very strange.

The next evening, I sketched out the bird-on-the-plaque image on a random piece of paper (see Appendix Four, p. 139). I have no idea if this image symbolized something, or it was a blend of images floating in my brain that coalesced as a dream. The paper I drew on was a meal delivery ticket, the kind that came with each of my meals.

The brown duck vision still baffles me today. It could have been a strange but meaningless hallucination. Perhaps I dozed off and had a snippet of an ephemeral dream. What symbolism can I attach to it—sitting duck, lame duck? And the shades of brown—drabness or vibrancy? Rather than assign some significance to the vision, I will let it be an enigma. Some other time its meaning may be revealed to me, but for the time being I'm happy to let it be a peculiar thing that happened on this journey.

That Monday morning was like every other morning—a wake-up poke in the arm from the phlebotomist tech for labs, the nurse's check of my temperature and blood pressure, the blood sugar finger-stick test, and an hour's wait before breakfast arrived. Still on a steady flow of oxygen, I passed the morning watching the first two hours of the Today show. My roommate Alfredo was preparing to be discharged and went through a series of phone calls setting up his ride home. In an upbeat mood, understandably, he cleaned himself up, got dressed, and then waited until a little past noon when he was wheeled out of the room. After his bed was changed and sanitized, I had the fond hope of being transferred to it, but that was not to be.

With Alfredo's departure, I had the room to myself for a short while, but I did not graduate to Bed A, which I had perceived as a better hospital bed. My time as the sole occupant of room 708 came to an end with the arrival of Pedro. Had I thought about it, I would have realized that beds would be in high demand given the number of COVID patients overwhelming the hospital. I was only a couple of days away from the War Zone, but the nurses told me it was still crowded with people seeking help.

Pedro was a nice man, more average in his appearance and demeanor than Alfredo. As we greeted each other he was reasonably preoccupied with his own medical needs. However, I did learn that he had been a hospital employee at one time. He had worked in the maintenance department until he retired two years ago. After he settled in, Pedro made frequent use of his cell phone, chatting with his family members who called or whom he phoned. I had my own thoughts and concerns so I simply minded my own business. Still, I could overhear half a conversation and understand those parts not in Spanish. Like most patients, he was relating his situation to his loved ones.

In the wee hours of the morning, as I was resting after my fifth and final Remdesivir treatment, something changed in Pedro's condition and the nursing staff tended to him without delay. Their presence and activity awakened me, and I kept to myself as I tried to surmise what was happening. A decision was made to move Pedro, perhaps for more advanced treatment or attention, and the room stirred with commotion for the time it took to enact the change. Naturally, nothing was said to me about his departure. I silently prayed for him, again grateful for the medical professionals who care for us patients.

By now I was well-practiced at using the bedside urinal at my disposal. It was certainly convenient in the middle of the night. I could sit on the edge of the bed or stand beside the bed to relieve myself, six or eight ounces at a time. This spared me the effort of wrangling the oxygen tubing and ever-present telemetry leads. Eventually, I learned to control the equipment that monitored me and helped me breathe.

Overnight between Monday and Tuesday, my fifth Remdesivir therapy had been administered, ending the course of treatment. About mid-morning, a new doctor, Dr. Habib Elghoul, introduced himself to me. He was concerned my lab work indicated that my lungs were not clearing as much as he had anticipated. The COVID had attached to my lungs so badly that I couldn't recover. They were also watching my liver function via the labs. This news was worrisome, but I adopted a wait and see attitude.

I was feeling minimally better, but the CT scan that would rule out a blood clot (a pulmonary embolism) had not happened yet, and I was still living on 15 L/per minute of oxygen. Dr. Elghoul ordered a second round of Remdesivir, pending what the CT scan revealed. This meant that I would receive five more treatments, and my stay in the hospital would be extended at least five more days.

Blog Entry #6—Setbacks
December 24, 2020

I suppose with any enterprise there are setbacks. This has certainly been true for me with COVID-19, and it becomes a matter of how you deal with them that gets your through the experience. To rule out the possibility that my recovery was not being prolonged due to a blood clot in my lungs—and I have a history of DVT[3] *blood clots—the doctor ordered a CT scan. It would be two days before this was completed.*

The first setback was finding someone to put a larger IV into my arm to accommodate the dye contrast they inject into you to do the scan. Without explaining this upfront, the tech was searching for a place to inject the IV needle. On his fourth try, he was successful, but I had to ask him, "Are you in?" Eleven hours had passed since the scan order was placed, and I was hoping this element of progress was a sign things were on the move.

For this scan to happen, three more things had to be in place: a wheelchair, an oxygen tank, and a medical transport team to monitor my heart and get me to the scan room. The night passed and nothing more happened. In the fiftieth hour [of my waiting] everything converged—in less than a half hour, the scan was accomplished and I was back in bed to await the results of the scan—another 15-hour wait.

These setbacks reveal an overloaded, overwhelmed medical system during [a] peak in the crisis. The bigger setback came when I learned the results of the CT scan. The first course (five doses) of the COVID-19 drug of choice had not done all it could to eliminate the COVID pneumonia from my body. This meant that I was in for an extended hospital stay of at least five more days. Medically, I understood what this meant and I quickly came to terms with it both emotionally and psychologically. Without being able to breathe on my own, I knew I wasn't ready to go home, nor did I want to go home and [possibly] have to return to the ER. Better stay where you are, have another round of the treatment, and receive the care being given to me.

Maybe setbacks are life's way of making a pause, re-evaluating, reassessing, revisiting, reviewing where you are and what your next steps are to be. Your life may depend on it.

Setbacks in business often involve something like a loss of revenue or a change in suppliers. In education an obstacle might be a required class that must be repeated. In a career it may be a promotion that doesn't materialize or a company downsize. People often have obstacles that cause them to veer off course and require them to reassess relationships. In a medical situation, a setback could be a course of treatment that is ineffective and prolongs a hospital stay, or worse, affects one's life.

Sue posted a new Facebook message on December 23, "Update on George: News not good. His lungs are badly damaged and not recovering,

3. DVT = Deep Vein thrombosis.

so doctor is starting him on another five days of Remdesivir." For days, Sue had been hearing from a lot of people as the wonder of social media carried the news.

ℰↄ⏅ↄℰ

Being a deathly ill patient was not a spiritually rich time for me. Hospitals are usually not conducive places for spiritual development, although when facing a medical crisis one's faith might be reexamined. As I think about it now, I entered the hospital with my usual attitude of taking life as it comes. Being a religious person, I draw from a well of faith that has sustained me in all of life's circumstances. We are never out of the providence of God's care, but that was being tested as my physical strength and upbeat attitude were diminishing.

People have asked me if I was afraid I was going to die. As I think back on the experience, I can't recall a moment when I felt my life was coming to an end. I knew my breathing was seriously compromised and I was weaker than at any other time in my life. When the reality of being a COVID patient hit home I felt discouraged. The doldrums of inactivity were hard to endure, but I never felt like I was about to "shuffle off this mortal coil," as in Hamlet's famous "To be or not to be" soliloquy. I have wondered if my first experience with Remdesivir, with its bright white light and vision of peering down at my body was a near-death experience. There was no voice saying anything, either to welcome me or send me back saying, "your time has not yet come." Who decides these things?

When I think about it now, I believe my natural reaction to a challenge is to study what is happening and learn from it. I was taught to trust medical professionals, and so I entrusted the care of my body to doctors and nurses who are trained to deal with disease. There's also a huge curiosity factor with me, which encourages me to ask questions, try to understand my condition, and do what I can to help myself. These aspects of my character were not immediately forthcoming, but as the days passed I could formulate my questions and do more than receive care. But I was certainly not there yet. Beneath this surface self-reflection is a strong will to live and not give up when things get rough, a conviction that still I have something to contribute to this life.

I can honestly say I had no crisis of faith with COVID. Does that mean I unconsciously take my faith for granted? Does it mean that I automatically lean on my faith in a trying time? Did I ignore or disregard any notion of my faith through this experience? I'm fond of Joan Baez's version of the spiritual which says, "Like a tree that's planted by the water I shall not be moved," echoing the words of Psalm 1:3.

Similarly, I take heart in the words of the refrain of Psalm 62, ". . . I shall not be shaken." Of course, moments of doubt have also shaped my faith. I've had times of uncertainty which have increased my yearning for the closeness of God's mercy, forgiveness and strength. With the psalmists I have prayed, "Why are you cast down, O my soul" (Psalm 42:5) and "Create in me a clean heart, O God" (Psalm 51:10). And I take solace in the invitation to "Give thanks to the Lord, for He is good, for His steadfast love endures forever." (Psalm 136 uses this as a refrain.).

Dave and Nikki

When a friend is laid up with an illness, many people want to reach out to help, do something that will ease the pain or help pass the time. Sue arranged for David and Nikki Holsinger to bring me a crossword puzzle book and a pair of pens. Sue did not ask for their help, they offered, and made clear that they would take care of it. Their effort would go a long way to relieve the tedium of the interminable hours as a patient. I was elated when the items were delivered to my room.

I immediately set to work solving the fifty puzzles from *The New York Times*. The 2002 book, edited by Will Shortz, contained Monday through Friday puzzles, ranging in difficulty from easy to tough. They were an especially welcome diversion in the middle of the night when I couldn't sleep or in the stretches between medical care. My energy level was improving. I can't say I was strong, but I could sit up for thirty minutes or so until I completed another puzzle. Between puzzles I would rest or stare out the window or watch television.

At some point Tuesday morning (before the puzzles arrived), I had a bout of diarrhea that I couldn't manage. I was moving toward the bathroom but I arrived too late. All I could do was stand there until I was empty. Rather than being embarrassed, I personally felt disappointed. I was also sorry for the nurse who cleaned me up. She did the job with professionalism and compassion, without making me feel bad or ashamed.

My Hospital Diet

While I was hospitalized, I was placed on a fifteen hundred-calorie, sixty grams of carbohydrate diabetic diet. The meal delivery ticket I used to sketch my wooden plaque "duck dream," reveals that I had a baked chicken breast, one cup of green beans, 2/3 cup of brown quinoa, a side salad with vinaigrette dressing, and a serving of fresh fruit. Generally speaking, the food portions were adequate but everything was so bland. Perhaps that was a sign that COVID had diminished my ability to taste and smell.

In a normal hospital stay, Kaiser offers "Room Service Dining." Because the hospital was slammed with COVID patients, the kitchen resorted to a few generic meals without the chance to make personal selections (even within a restricted diet). The dinner entrees rotated between baked chicken breast, turkey meatloaf, and portabella mushroom ravioli, each served with lo carb sides and fruit.

Lunches consisted of tomato, chicken, or vegetable soup, with a dinner roll on the side, accompanied by 1% milk or, if I was lucky, fruit juice. At breakfast, a scrambled egg, dry toast, a piece of fruit—banana, apple, or orange—or a fruit cup of fruit cocktail, diced peaches, or diced pears. I could wash that down with low-fat milk, coffee or hot tea while missing my daily ration of Diet Coke.

I grew extremely tired of the grayish turkey meatloaf and the paste-like portabella mushroom filling of the ravioli. All I had to spice them was a small picnic packet of salt or pepper. The treat I gave myself for making it through one of those distasteful meals was to eat the fruit cup last. That gave my taste buds something to look forward to and lifted my spirits. By far the most intolerable thing was the chamomile tea they brought with dinner. It tasted like water poured through dirty socks!

I was pleased to receive cold cereal one morning, and a couple of days a serving of oatmeal was delivered. Another day I got a meager breakfast bowl of potato, scrambled egg and cheese with a small banana for "dessert." These meals were a welcome change, and I wondered if the kitchen had made a mistake.

Back at home, with Matt testing positive for COVID-19, Sue also thought it wise to be tested. She had already suspended her volunteer work until she could get a testing appointment. There was no sense risking others' health and lives in case she was an asymptomatic carrier.

On December 22, she went to the testing site at the University of Redlands, about a mile from home. She reported that there was a large number of people being tested, and she waited an hour and a half as the line snaked around University Hall. Two days later, she got her result—negative. The way she put it, "I was too mean to catch COVID." With this good news, Sue returned on Christmas Day to serve lunches with the RCRC.

✑✐

I don't know precisely when it happened, but I came to a roadblock that I could not get beyond. Sometime before my second round of Remdesivir treatments, I was stunned to discover I no longer had any reserves upon which to draw. It had been several days since I could remember praying for myself or for those around me. I was aware that others were praying for me, but it seemed like I didn't know how to formulate a prayer. My daily habit of regular prayer appeared nonexistent. My well of faith had run dry.

Under normal circumstances I can reason my way through a problem. I commonly respond to life's ups and downs with an emotional balance and sense of resolve. My patience has often seen me through my challenges. When something is difficult I've been known to research an appropriate way to deal with it. It's not unusual for me to draw on hymn texts with their rich metaphors or familiar prayers or ritual texts to help me cope. A relatively quick wit and sense of humor are constant companions.

All of these resources had vanished in that moment. My mind went blank. I could not form words or keep a thought in my head. I was grasping for something beyond my reach. I was completely empty—mentally, emotionally, spiritually empty. Later, when I had recovered the ability to pray, I reflected on this phenomenon. I pieced together what I had experienced and added another entry to my blog. It was the lowest point of my hospitalization and one that left me completely drained.

Blog Entry #5—Where Prayer Ends
December 22, 2020

In the solitude of COVID-19, I discovered where prayer ends. Maybe the words are the first thing to go anyway, but they do go away. The most familiar words may come to mind, but they hold no meaning and don't bring comfort. "Thy will be done," always a good prayer, evaporated. "God be merciful to me, a sinner," [it] may be true but doesn't seem to apply in this void. "Jesus, remember me". . . not yet. Your search for words to string together to express how you feel just ends—no sense of frustration, no remorse, not a bit of embarrassment. The words are just gone.

Deeper in this shadow, you've given up on words, you look for the faces of the people you know who pray. And guess what, they're not there either. My mother taught me to pray—she's gone. I've prayed with dozens of friends and colleagues—I couldn't feel one of you. The further you recess into this abyss you lose the energy to find a course correction. You get overwhelmed by the bleak terrain you're in. Every "where" seems to lead to a dead end. You can't find the strength to ask, "What's wrong with me?"

In the back of my mind I think of the prayers that are the sighs too deep for words, but I find no comfort there in this dark place of my heart. I recall the hymn, and I quote it to myself:

> *"As o'er each continent and island,*
> *the dawn leads on another day,*
> *the voice of prayer is never silent,*
> *nor die the strains of praise away."[4]*

Who is praying for me today? My voice is silent. I cannot pray. I don't even want to try. The darkness grows.

Beyond these hospital walls, I am told that a world of people are praying for me. Voices from many corners of my life are worried about me, and I am grateful for their concern. I know that prayers are being lifted, and I hope they find a receptive ear in the divine. They need to pray; I can't.

I could not pray. That was a stunning moment for a preacher, one who is (as we jokingly used to say) "paid to pray." To echo a *Christian Century* contributor, I couldn't pray, but maybe my writing became my prayer.[5] The mantle of my professional life seemed so distant. This is not a source of shame for me, just the honest truth of my experience. I've thought a lot about my inability to pray in the midst of my illness. I've wondered, what good is a pastor who can't pray? But every pastor is also a human being and there are moments when we hit a wall, and I was there.

At the least, prayer is a list of requests brought before God in the expectation that they will be met. Sometimes we end our prayers "in the name of Jesus," as if that were a magic formula. At best, prayer is deep spiritual communion between the soul and God. There are nuances of formality, style, intensity, and language to our prayers, including being present to

4. *The United Methodist Hymnal,* #690.
5. Thomas, "My Mother's Gift of Words," 37.

one another in silence. The variety of prayers in the Bible remind me that no subject is beyond addressing in prayer. When I was running on empty, the resources I normally rely on felt absent or out of reach. That is not an indicator of a lack of faith, but a sign of my weakness in the moment. I also see it as a measure of my complete trust in the God who sustains me in all of life's circumstances.

The day after I wrote the "Where Prayer Ends" blog, my pastor, J.T. Greenleaf, phoned in the afternoon. He knew about the "no visitors" policy and Sue had kept him informed of my status. On my behalf, Sue was reluctant to give him my room phone number. She relented when he said he only wanted to pray with me. I was still having difficulty controlling my breathing and could only form a few words at a time. J.T. asked to pray with me and then offered a prayer. After he prayed, I told him through my erratic breathing and spontaneous tears, "You don't know what this means to me."

When I wrote my "Where Prayer Ends" blog, I was also thinking of the city of people who serve as the staff of the hospital, all contributing their talents, skills and labor to patient care.

In the non-solitude of COVID-19, I discovered the array of people who are elements in your experience. The nurses are the regulars, tending to your needs, answering your questions, focused on treating you. There are the EVS techs who empty the trash, mop the floors, clean up your spills. Several floors below where you lie [there are] cooks, nutritionists, meal assembly workers, clean-up crews, food delivery people so you get three meals a day.

Closer at hand are the pharmacists, who fulfill prescriptions, provide the dosage cleared by the doctors, so you not only get the therapeutics for your illness, but the daily meds you would be taking at home from Metformin to Lipitor. Hospital administrators also play their role in hiring qualified staff (at all levels), balancing staff workloads with the demand COVID-19 has made on the health care system. Even in all these roles, the darkness of the pandemic hovers, putting all at risk and challenging the very fabric that you in your darkness as a patient are trying to survive.

Blog Entry #5—Where Prayer Ends

My third roommate, José, arrived mid-afternoon. Immediately I felt sorry for this unfortunate man. He was large, corpulent—I estimated about three hundred and fifty pounds—and he could not stand on his own. When I got out of bed to use the bathroom, I could see beyond the curtain separating our beds. His bed was lowered significantly, and it seemed that his weight was causing the bed to fold in upon itself.

As when I first arrived in the room, José had greatly labored breathing. I soon learned he was a kidney dialysis patient with treatment sessions lasting a long time during a twenty-four-hour stretch. As the treatment either began or finished, the staff attending to José would talk him through his needs and comfort level.

Because of his size and infirmity, José could not get himself to the bathroom. Whenever he needed to relieve himself he would call the nurses, and the hubbub of getting him situated created quite a ruckus. On more than one occasion, José couldn't find the call button, or it was out of his reach, and he asked me to get their attention. His efforts did not always produce immediate results, and his moans and groans added to the noise level. Discussions with the medical staff happened at an increased volume, making it hard to rest or sleep for long.

By this point in my stay at Kaiser—seven days in—I knew the lay of the land and the patterns of the day. This included the location of the TV remote control. In a room designed for one patient, the remote was not long enough to easily reach my side of the room—just enough to reach the foot of my bed. In a friendly way I negotiated the control of the remote for the evening news and Jeopardy. This kept me occupied for about three hours.

When I had hogged the remote long enough, I passed it over to José. His choice of television programming included *La Rosa de Guadalupe*. This Mexican anthology drama series airs on Univision. Each episode tells an inspirational story, where the protagonists overcome great obstacles thanks to their faith. The stories concern people with problems who invoke the help of the Virgin Mary, and where a rose appears and their problems are solved. The TV-14 rated show debuted in 2008 and has filmed nearly 1,000 episodes. Ratings for this show are generally low (2.7 out of 10), but it is highly regarded among young adults. I was able to catch enough of the Spanish dialogue to follow the plotline.

Either because José couldn't find the remote or was too incapacitated to bother, the TV was later tuned into the show *Chrisley Knows Best*. An American reality television series airing on USA Network, the show centers on an Atlanta millionaire real estate developer, his wife and their children, who exude Southern charm. They have anything money can buy but face everyday problems with major drama. Chrisley, the father, runs his life and family with an iron fist, a micromanaging control freak. The TV-14 rated show debuted in 2014 to mixed reviews. Like most of so-called "reality" television, the show is a complete waste of time.

José either preferred to keep the TV on all night, or he fell asleep without turning it off, and one night was particularly challenging. A series of infomercials on the 1980s ran for five hours, documenting each year of the decade in thirty-minute segments. The announcer's droning voice was not soothing and was interrupted every seven minutes to inform the viewer how to order the DVD set. Having had no quality sleep, at 4:00 I located the remote (under José's pillow) and changed the channel to the morning news and NBC's TODAY Show which followed. Somehow I survived that dreadful night with short periods of dozing and giving attention to my own needs for some kind of comfort.

Despite the television disruption, I tried to sleep on my stomach for the first time during my hospital stay. This had been recommended for COVID patients, but the staff had not made this suggestion to me. It was extremely uncomfortable for me, but I got snatches of sleep in a three-hour period, awaking when a new year of the eighties infomercial was announced on the TV.

Christmas Eve

When Dr. Casimiro visited me later that morning, he gave me the results of the CT scan: the good news that there was no blood clot in my lungs. However, my left lung was pretty occluded, and COVID pneumonia was covering more than half of my right lung, justifying a second round of Remdesivir treatments. I was still receiving 15 L/min. of oxygen. I asked about the C-PAP machine Dr. Casimiro had ordered earlier, and he said he'd check into it. Christmas Eve was also the day I wrote the "Setbacks" blog, reflecting on the CT scan experience.

Due to the gap between the end of my first round of Remdesivir and the beginning of my second round of the drug, I was put on a new timetable treatment. The Remdesivir would be administered in the early afternoon—1:30 or 2:00 pm instead of the middle of the night. I was able to make it through the morning, have lunch, and then receive the hour-long IV-drip therapy.

Although I still braced myself for the treatment, it was less stressful somehow in the daylight. Having spent a fair number of days in my hospital bed, I had learned how to place my body in a comfortable position. When the drugs started to enter my system, I closed my eyes and tried to doze off, or at least rest, while it happened. By now I also had a sense of what to expect.

Maybe the daylight or the other noises in the room were distractions, but the effects of the drugs seemed less intense. Perhaps I was feeling stronger in general as my hospital stay was prolonged. I'm sure that my attitude changed from simply tolerating the medical treatment to accepting the course of care the doctors were giving me. Instead of just receiving the medication, I was asking how this was going to help me.

With the darkness of the day's end, I tuned in to the evening news and caught glimpses of reports on worship services being held in various churches in the Los Angeles area. A week before I became sick I had begun planning a virtual Christmas Eve service for Trinity Lutheran Church. I drafted a "Lessons and Carols" format to celebrate the Feast of the Incarnation. My plan included a brief homily that I would have recorded ahead of time. As I have done in previous years, the service would review the Biblical story from prophecy to the manger interspersed with familiar hymns and Scripture readings.

From my hospital bed I thought of how those plans remained in my computer files. The warm emotions of that service might not be experienced, and I wondered what the church would do instead. They had the invitation and the option to worship with a neighboring church, but I let those thoughts evaporate. I still don't know how they celebrated the occasion. Of course, I would have been in church somewhere that evening if not for my condition. It was a Christmas Eve unlike any other I had ever experienced.

Lying there, trying to fall asleep with my troubled breathing, I quietly recited phrases from my favorite Christmas hymns. "How silently, how silently the wondrous gift is given, so God imparts to human hearts the blessings of his heaven . . ." (from "O Little Town of Bethlehem"). Phillips Brooks' third verse is one of the most concise, poetic and theological statements of the Incarnation that I have ever seen. This was followed by "What can I give him, poor as I am?" and the closing part of that verse "what I can I give him: give him my heart." I am particularly fond of Dan Fogelberg's version of this 1872 Christina G. Rossetti hymn, "In the Bleak Midwinter." I certainly felt my own form of bleakness in this wintry moment but held on to the hymn's final thought which brought me a measure of comfort that night. I drifted off to sleep before I could finish thinking about "Son of God, love's pure light . . ." (from "Silent Night"). I couldn't sing, of course, so the hymns sang to me, and in a small way my heart found a way to worship.

Why were these carols my choices? They are favorites, yes, easy to remember, and comforting in their tenderness. What I had been missing was not only the traditional activities of Christmas Eve, but also the Scripture phrases I've heard all my life. *"For a child has been born for us, a son given to us . . ." (Isaiah 9:6),* and *"Do not be afraid; for see—I am bringing you good news of great joy . . ." (Luke 2:10).* While I was hospitalized, no one read them to me, said them to me, or sang them to me.

Only in my memories could I be bathed in such holy reflection. Instead, I leaned on the musical language of my spirit to bring the nativity of the Lord to my bedside. Ever so gently, elements of my faith were replenished and renewed in the remembered verses of those lullabies.

Christmas Day

For most of us, I suspect, Christmas Day has a certain pattern that we follow every year. In our house, once a cup of coffee or tea is into us, we go about the ritual of opening gifts from our loved ones. Breakfast is usually followed with phone calls to or from relatives who live at a distance. The rest of the day develops with family time, meal preparations or other casual events as we celebrate the holiday. This familiar and comforting pattern helps us treasure every Christmas.

Prior to COVID-19, the most unusual Christmas Day I had ever experienced came when we lived in Kona, Hawaii. On Christmas that year, Sue and I flew from Kona to Honolulu for a meeting with our bishop to talk about a possible change of appointment. Neither of us had ever flown anywhere on Christmas day for any reason. Even during the experience we talked about how unusual it was.

On Christmas day in the hospital I was awake before dawn and watched the sunrise through my hospital window. I was ready for the lab technician when she came to draw blood at 6:30 and prepared for the nurse to read my vital signs. The day was unfolding like every other day in the hospital.

I had determined that I was going to ask for a bath or shower. It had been too long since I had felt clean. I knew it was time, past time really. My timing had to be right, however. I needed to find the moment when I could make my request without throwing the nurses' routine off-kilter. After breakfast, I looked the nurse straight in the eye and as kindly as I could asked for a bath. Later I wrote about the experience in my blog.

My COVID Crucible

On Christmas Day I received two presents that made the day a bit brighter and unique, even in this situation. The first gift was a bath. I had the presence of mind to plan for it, and I would have done it myself if I hadn't been offered the help I accepted. [While I was seated on the side of the bed, the nurse added warm water to a pouch of pre-soaped sponges; the cleansing solution evaporated on use.]

As the water flowed over my head, I was overcome with emotion. No shame or embarrassment; not helplessness either. What my heart connected to was a faith memory from the 1980s. My mother came to a footwashing service during Holy Week and I washed her feet. Her tears flowed that evening thinking of all the times she had bathed me, and here I was bathing her. In an instant, that memory flooded over me and I wept. The remainder of that bath produced a deep sense of relief. It had been about 10 days since my last shower.

After my bath, the day felt infinitely better. I had a new lease on life and a much improved disposition. We often take for granted the simple act of bathing ourselves. I think of homeless people who do not have this basic need met on any regular basis. I can't remember going more than a day or two without a shower—much less the ten days I had just faced. I deeply appreciated and will often recall this treasured Christmas Day experience.

You'll note that I have not mentioned having any visitors. Normally, the appearance of visitors brightens any patient's hospitalization. But no visitors were allowed on the COVID ward (the whole seventh floor), and only the hospital staff were allowed in the rooms. Numerous media reports of patients dying alone or being separated from loved ones during their hospital stay were reminders of the "no visitors" policy and did not come as a surprise to me. Still, it would have been wonderful to have Sue with me.

The remainder of the day was pretty ordinary. I worked a couple of crosswords and talked with Sue. All I had to report was that there was no change in my progress, I was showing no improvement. That did not mean the treatments were not working (according to Dr. Casimiro), but that the virus was running its course. I was still receiving 15 L/min. of oxygen. I told Sue about my bath and the good lunch I'd had. Christmas dinner was a memorable meal, described in my blog.

The second gift of Christmas Day was a slice of cherry pie with a beef tenderloin lunch. It was such a wonderful treat to have a different meal, but the pie proved to be costly. Most patients, repeated the nurses, saw a spike in their blood sugar count, and doses of insulin were required to restore equilibrium.

Blog Entry #8—Christmas Day

Another thing that made this Christmas Day unusual was that I watched a football game and a basketball game on TV—both choices José had made. Those who know me well know that I don't care for football or have much use for basketball, let alone taking the time to watch them on TV. I also had my seventh Remdesivir treatment; it was almost becoming routine.

I also made a point of chatting with each of the staff members who came into my room about their Christmas events. Maybe I was feeling better and taking a greater interest in others rather than wallowing in my own misery. This change of attitude was also noted in my blog.

Feelings of gratitude have begun to surface in the last couple of days. When I have had the strength, opportunity and presence of mind, I have tried to express my gratitude to each nurse, lab tech, EVS or other medical helpers who have assisted me along this journey. In some cases I have witnessed their compassionate care toward others; in other moments, I have been the recipient.

When possible, I have complimented their gifts of communication, tender loving care and empathy for the needs of others. Especially in the face of the COVID-19 pandemic, the risks they take and the sacrifices they are making—personally and professionally—cannot be overstated. Gratitude seems such an inadequate word for such an enormous gift.

Blog Entry #8—Christmas Day

Twice near the end of my stay in Room 708-B, I was awake in the middle of the night, unable to sleep and stir-crazy idle as I sat up in bed. I asked if there was a spare fruit cup around. No, but I was given two containers of sugar-free Jell-O. There are many hours between a 5:30 pm dinner and an 8:30 am breakfast. I savored these servings of Jell-O like they were my favorite flavor of ice cream or a meal of steak and lobster. It's amazing how such a simple thing eased my anxiety over not sleeping. Comfort food, indeed.

Hospital Room Window

I was so grateful that I had the bed close to the window in our room. My bed was positioned at a 90° angle to the window beyond my head, my feet pointing toward the interior door. The window gave me a plate-glass view of the world beyond Room 708-B. When I learned I was allowed to raise the window shade it became part of my daily routine. I would raise the shade at first light and gaze out on the early movements of the public. I could watch the sun rise above the mountains to the east and observe the night's shadows as they disappeared.

Having lived in Southern California's Inland Empire for many years, I was aware of the landmarks and other features around the hospital. I knew the street names, where the freeway curved, what cities were nearby. I could see, imagine, and sense the world I knew outside. Every day I studied the view before me.

My curiosity kicked in, and I began to imagine that my home in Redlands was due east of my hospital room in Fontana. There was no way I could see that far away, an eighteen-mile distance. Yet I had a strong, recurring feeling that I could draw a straight line from here to there. I wished I had a drone to fly or the skills to chart the course between the hospital and my home. Maybe it was a longing to be home that fueled my thoughts, but I knew I would never know.

Still, the activity seven floors below me was intriguing. I didn't spend a great deal of time peering out the window, but each time I spent a few moments there, I felt a bit rhapsodic about all I surveyed. I could see rooftops and driveways, and I observed people coming to the medical clinic buildings, staff members coming to work. Businesses were opening up for the day's commerce, and I watched the traffic on Valley Blvd. There were passing trains along the nearby Union Pacific rail lines, and an occasional plane on approach to Ontario International Airport.

I recall thinking about all of the places I had been and the experiences I've had in the broader area I was surveying. Fifty years of memories came drifting in: my student days at the University of Redlands, my first marriage, an early job in Colton. Recollections of adventures and misadventures came to mind along with the faces of former friends and acquaintances. My parents both had been heart patients at Loma Linda. I thought of the years of Annual Conference at the U of R, and how my church youth work and two church appointments all took place in the area within my sight through that window. More recent and happier thoughts of our home and the activities of our retirement quickly took over my nostalgic reflections.

The glimpses and ideas floated through my mind and gave me something to mull over other than the sorry situation I was enduring. I could think of better things than the COVID pandemic and my erratic breathing.

That hospital window became a friend of sorts, and before I left the hospital I mapped out what I saw and what I imagined. The distant mountains were always present, and I was glad the atmosphere was clear enough to see them. I sketched the hospital compound and estimated I was 750' above the ground (see Appendix Three, p. 137). I noted the position of the moon and where the sun rose. I could see some water towers and the buildings I presumed were the Loma Linda University Hospital. My drawing included the Union Pacific rail line to the south and the approximate location of the San Bernardino Airport. On my crude map, I drew what I imagined was the straight line between the hospital and my home, but short of a formal survey of the area, I wouldn't know how far off my idea might be. The window proved to be a good diversion.

Dr. Elghoul returned and announced that my lab work had been good. He decided it was time to reduce my oxygen from 15 L/min. to 10 L/min., a sure sign of progress. On his order, I was given a smaller mask, and he said I needed to work my way to 95% oxygen saturation while breathing on my own, weaning me off so much oxygen. He also ordered oxygen for me at home, which was an indicator that I might be discharged soon. Dr. Elghoul further explained how the second round of Remdesivir therapy was all that could be administered, and there was no other treatment they could offer, yet another sign that my hospital stay was nearing its end.

Because of Dr. Elghoul's order, Sue had talked with Apria Healthcare, a provider of durable medical equipment. She arranged for oxygen to be delivered to our home. We were fortunate that Apria was able to supply oxygen to us because I was a Kaiser patient, and they were only doing business with Kaiser. The equipment would be delivered the following day and be at the ready when I came home. The equipment would include a portable oxygen tank to help facilitate my eventual transport home, and an oxygen concentrator that I would use to provide continuous oxygen flow as I moved around the house with several yards of plastic hose.

I became concerned about the cost of my hospitalization, and Sue talked with Melissa, a case manager assigned to me. She told Sue that the daily rate was $200 for my level of coverage after a $4,000 deductible, and

I could see the dollar signs adding up when Sue told me. She was also told that the 20 percent co-pay was being waived for COVID patients, and that made me feel a little bit better.

Another insurance issue was causing me concern, one that began a week before I became sick. Health insurance plans are often renewed or re-evaluated in the last few months of the year, especially for Medicare recipients. Due to a change in how my health insurance was being handled, I had started working with VIA Benefits, an insurance brokerage company doing business with the United Methodist Board of Pensions to arrange my future health insurance coverage.

My inability to resolve this matter before my COVID journey left a bit of unfinished business on the table. The end of the year drawing near meant there was a looming deadline to be met. Sue tried to help by contacting VIA Benefits and the human resource director at the California-Pacific Conference. However, she could not enact any changes on my behalf. It would be up to me to complete the arrangements when business opened on Monday, two days away.

As a Kaiser COVID patient, I knew I wanted to keep my insurance coverage intact as much as possible. I surmised that I would have some sort of COVID follow-up care, I liked my primary care provider and my podiatrist, and I knew I would have a two-year follow-up appointment with Dr. Lee, who had done my knee replacement surgery in 2019. Kaiser would be the coverage for me, and I thought I could resolve this issue when I got home in a couple of days.

Another Remdesivir treatment was on the afternoon's agenda, so I found my comfortable position and prepared for the medication. I didn't write about it until the morning I left the hospital, but these thoughts were on my mind:

Blog Entry #9—Medication
December 29, 2020

How did my presents come wrapped this Christmas? Pretty paper and bows did not seem to exist in my mind; boxes, bags and stockings were mere far-off ideas that came and went with the moments. Shopping, wrapping and plans for a Christmas celebration were interrupted by the disease that left no room for preparation.

. . . I began to think about the medication differently. Rather than brace myself, I began to say, "Let this be a healing balm for my body. Course through

my system and cleanse my lungs of this pneumonia. Bring my body rest and recovery; let there be health and wholeness." Those final three treatments were equally challenging, but more tolerable than the first seven had been.

Beyond these disease-specific meds, I was given my usual daily prescriptions and checked for blood sugar (multiple times a day!), given blood thinner (Lovenox) and when necessary, insulin—a protocol that replaced the use of metformin.

December 26

The day after Christmas was filled with activity, but it was also a reflective day for me. Maybe it was the small steps of progress I was making, the strength that was returning to my body, or some other unknown element of my care, but I thought about where I was, what I had gone through, and what lay ahead.

These ideas of how I had progressed and what healing may have started in me gave me the first sense of hope I had allowed myself to feel. The worst was over and there was a future of recovery from the virus. I wasn't ready to get up and dance but I could perceive a time when I would go home. This joyous thought seemed to match the holy day that was upon us. Before long I was feeling gratitude for my care and marveling at the medical science that had put me on this trajectory.

Blog Entry #7—The Road Not Taken
December 26, 2020

Robert Frost's famous poem, "The Road Not Taken," has been drifting through my mind—especially the part that mentions the dark and deep woods, and the miles to go before I sleep lines.[6] *The poem is deceptively simple and more profound the more you ponder it. The fancy word is multivalent. As I rest, I think of the deep darkness I have been experiencing, how over-whelming it has seemed, and what this challenge means to me going forward.*

Going forward may seem like words of hope, some level of improvement in my outlook, or some sense of light at the end of the tunnel. Elements of these ideas come to the surface every now and then, but do not linger and disappear as quickly as they arrive. That's where the "miles to go" stakes its claim.

---

6. Frost, "The Road Not Taken."

When I was first diagnosed as COVID-19 positive, I was determined not to be a statistic [of course, I was already]. Yes, I was one of the new cases among the 52,281 that day; I went on to be one of the 16,426 hospitalizations. What I did not fathom [was] being one of the 28,538 fatalities from this pandemic. My goal was (and is) to be among those who are the recoveries—again light at the end of the tunnel, but without knowing how long, dark and deep this darkness would be.[7]

Are there other signs I should be noticing? A second round of drugs promises improvement. Better sleep at night is another minor indicator—not without interruptions, but with incremental length and frequency. My appetite is good, even if the food choices are less than ideal for my palate. Repetition may be easy for the kitchen crew, but the tedium of the meals is exasperating. I can understand limited portions, carb and sugar control, calorie counts and many of the elements that make for a controlled diabetic diet. Knowing how slammed the hospital census is gives me a bit of patience and tolerance. Maybe that glimpse into my own minimal compassion is another sign that I am on the mend. Besides, my oxygen saturation level is staying strong with a lowered amount of oxygen being administered. But there are miles to go.

Sue's Facebook message for this day reveals a note of hope: "Here's the good news! They have reduced George's oxygen use from 15 liters a minute to 10 liters and reduced the size face mask he is wearing. Two more doses of Remdesivir to go, but his lab work is good. Thank you so much for your prayers." Prayer groups in several places had added their voices to the mix of those praying for me.

Beyond my thoughts of Frost's poetry, I pondered the appalling numbers of people who were taken ill or had died from this disease. It was staggering to me. In my imagination, those affected by COVID-19, at every level of our society, felt like a tsunami of devastation. At the same time, how easy it has been to have our eyes glaze over and not think about the lives behind the statistics. These are hardly the reflections of a Christmas season, but they were my thoughts on Boxing Day.

December 27

I had now reached my eleventh day in the hospital. I was using less oxygen and finding it easier to sustain my breathing. Sometime during the day

7. https://covid19.ca.gov/state-dashboard/

my oxygen intake was decreased from 10 L/min. to 4 L/min. The skin on my arms and stomach was discolored by all the blood drawn for lab work, blood sugar testing, and shots of insulin and Lovenox I had endured. I was becoming quite adept at getting myself to the bathroom and back into bed without getting tangled up in wires and tubes. I had been around long enough to see compassionate nurses for a second time. For the most part, their caring nature and professionalism made our encounters pleasant, and focused on the business at hand.

This was now my second Sunday in the hospital. I remember asking if there was a Sunday paper on sale in the hospital gift shop, but I had no real hope I could get hold of one. I has some cash in my wallet, stuffed in the pocket of my jeans, and I would have paid two to three times the newsstand cost for a paper.

I had changed into a hospital gown days earlier (and had it changed once or twice), and my clothes had been folded into a plastic bag for patient belongings. In addition to the clothing I had worn to the hospital, the bag contained the underwear Sue brought me (now just laundry), the cell phone charger, my crossword puzzle book, pens and my odd assortment of writing papers containing my blog entries. Two or three times a day, I reached into the bag for one of its items or to check that the bag's contents were secure.

Sue and I surely talked on the phone sometime during the day, but none of her notes bear that date so there wasn't any new medical news to tell her. I know that I wrote down the information I needed to call VIA Benefits the following day. I used part of the day to draw a simple map of the world outside my window. The day also brought my ninth Remdesivir treatment, almost a welcome part of the day. The notion of going home was floating around in my mind, so Sue and I shared ideas about how to accomplish it.

Sue may not have been able to visit me in the hospital, but she was with me every step of the way. Her skills in managing arrangements eased my mind and made each transition smooth—truly a gift of her love.

My hospitalization left Sue in charge of everything at home. All the daily chores she normally took care of were coupled with the tasks I would have done. I'm sure it was similar to those times I have traveled from home without her. She is good at managing her time and pragmatic enough to know what needs to be done and when. In our telephone exchanges I never heard a word of complaint. I'm sure that the household chores were the least of her worries, but this was another reminder of how profoundly blessed I am to have her in my life.

As the days continued Sue had her own concerns to handle. Matt had tested positive for COVID, and he needed the care she provides to help him cope. She took food and medicine to his apartment and gave what comfort she could. No mother wants to see her children suffer.

If Sue felt any self-concern, it did not stop her compassionate response to others. Her voice never wavered and her attitude remained positive and hopeful. She was eager to hear about my care, no matter how little things changed. She translated what was happening with me into updates she gave to all who phoned or messaged her on Facebook. She was a steadfast rock throughout my COVID experience.

December 28

The weather forecast on the evening news predicted the following day would be rather cloudy and cooler with a shower, and they were right. December 28 arrived with "brief but heavy downpours through the afternoon."[8] The *Redlands Daily Facts*, quoting the National Weather Service, noted that Ontario recorded 1.3 inches of rain. The storm also brought snow to the local mountains, a delight for anyone willing to put chains on their car and drive up to play in the winter wonderland. Although I like doing this every four or five years, I'm usually content to see the snow-capped peaks from the valley floor.

That morning, when I opened the window shade in my room, I saw the raindrops on the glass and effects of the rain on the wet streets below. It was a welcome sight, and I had a few moments of delight as I studied the vision before me. Rain is not exactly rare in southern California, but infrequent enough to be remarkable when it appears. I am always glad to see the rain. It usually makes me feel pensive and poetic.

This time was no exception, but my contemplation did not become poetic expression. My thoughts were more immediate—about how the rain is such a blessing and how clean everything looks after it has been rain-washed. The rain can also bring a sense of melancholy, and I remember feeling a brief moment of self-pity.

In the lull after breakfast, following the usual medical attention given me at dawn, I initiated what would be a ninety-minute series of

8. *Redlands Daily Facts*, December 29, A-1.

conversations with the folks at VIA Benefits. I had planned to handle the business of selecting my health care coverage for the new year when I got home, but time was running out. This kind of transaction is not so simple or easily completed. In addition to being time-consuming, it can also try my patience.

The first person I talked to was the one who assesses the call's purpose. After about fifteen minutes of primary questions and self-identification verification, I was put in touch with a licensed benefits counselor whose job it was to lay out the multiple options for my health insurance decisions. This also involved a second round of authentication to affirm my identity, a step that requires twice the time it took to get to this point. I had now invested forty-five minutes in this call, so I had to keep going or start the process again from the beginning.

Round three began with another proof of identity and the confirmation of the plan I had chosen. But I was not finished yet. The third person was the actual agent who could seal the deal. To do this, the agent had to read every disclaimer and nuance of the coverage choice I made. After one final recap of the entire business, I was given a confirmation number. Gratefully, I was finished.

Everyone involved in this procedure was cordial, polite, and professional. They must be hired for their ability to remain calm on the phone. Each employee advised me they were recording the transaction, with my permission, "for training purposes." I needed the insurance coverage and the patience of Job to get through this process. I started off as pleasantly as I could, but my tolerance for the minutiae and ability to follow every detail grew thinner with each minute.

It would be one thing to be calling from the comfort of home, but I was phoning from a hospital bed, plugged into an oxygen port, tired from my twelfth day of COVID discomfort, and straining to keep my wits about me as I talked with the disembodied, far-away voices. Ugh! I didn't want the VIA Benefits people to know I am in the hospital. I was using the room phone to conduct my business and worried that the hospital operator would interrupt my lengthy call, wondering why I've tied up the line.

Midway through this telephone ordeal, my roommate José (remember him?) was having some kind of crisis of his own. The ensuing noise level as the nurses attended to him made it hard to hear all the detail I am supposed to be absorbing. With José taken care of, a bit of calm was restored and I breathed a sigh of relief. I was thrilled when my call was finished without the doctor coming in to see me or any more calamities interrupting.

There was just enough time to use the bathroom before Dr. Elghoul made his brief daily appearance. I would have my tenth and final Remdesivir treatment that afternoon; then it was possible I would be going home the following day. That is always a patient's favorite news. I was relieved to hear this, of course, but even more relieved that I had settled my health insurance business. My morning had been both frustrating and exhausting, even though satisfactory.

Right after the doctor's visit, I called Sue to report the news of my possible hospital release. Dr. Elghoul had dropped my oxygen from 4 L/min. to 2 L/min. and encouraged me to move around today. If I did well during the day and overnight, I might go home. I also related the outcome of the VIA Benefits call and gave her the confirmation number.

Before Dr. Elghoul left, I made a final attempt to get a C-PAP machine for my last night in the hospital. I reminded him that one had been ordered several days earlier, but it had never appeared. He misunderstood my request and ordered a C-PAP machine to be delivered through Apria at a cost of $194.45 (my 20 percent co-pay). This set off a series of phone calls to resolve the confusion. Sue was told that Apria ordered the exact same C-PAP unit that I had received in 2017.

What we needed was an adapter for connecting the machine I already owned to the oxygen converter that Apria had delivered. I asked Sue to refuse any attempt to deliver a new C-PAP machine, and I told the folks at Apria that I would refuse pay for one if they delivered it. I was frustrated that a C-PAP never appeared, miffed that the doctor misunderstood my request, and angry that Apria would so cavalierly send a new machine my way. Eventually, we were able to communicate our need and they agreed to send us the adapter and a picture illustrating how to install it.

Everything was set for my return home . . . almost. We still had to work out how I would be transported home and how my car, parked in the Kaiser garage for two weeks, would make it home. Sue arranged with my sister, Mary, and her husband, Terry, to help get me home. This meant a series of phone calls when they were enjoying a day in snowy Idyllwild.

❧⌔❧

My last night in the hospital was quite memorable. It was bedtime, and I was preparing to call it a day when a nurse came in and introduced himself to me, "I'm Bonaventure!" If he said his last name, I didn't catch it, or it didn't stay with me. He was more informal than most of the nurses I had met, but he appeared in full PPE. I thought it odd that there would be a shift change at that time of night. Shortly, Bonaventure made it clear that he was a nurse, but not *my* nurse. He was in my room to make a social call, my first and only visitor!

Bonaventure is the adopted son of an Orange County couple who had heard about me through our friend, Dan Gara, who had read about my illness via one of Sue's Facebook posts. Still surprised by his visit, it took a couple of repetitions before I understood the connection. Bonaventure told his story of coming to the United States from Ghana. This couple had supported him as he got his education. They were members of the church where Dan attends, and they had been praying for me. They connected the dots when they thought of how their son worked in the same hospital where I was a patient. (I presume they asked him to visit me.) Some might look at this as a wonderful coincidence. I choose to think of it as the intricate interweaving of the Holy Spirit in our lives as people of faith.

As our visit continued, we learned a little about each other. Bonaventure is married to a doctor with UC Riverside who trains residents in family practice at its Community Clinic in Moreno Valley. I marveled at the way he and his wife put themselves at risk to work with COVID patients. I told him how stunned I was that he would take the time to visit me when he could have gone home at the end of his workday. It was as if he had appeared to me as an angel, a messenger from God to bless me as I was headed home.

Bonaventure's faith was clearly evident from his language and the kind attention he was showing me. I presumed he knew I was a pastor, or maybe that was a perception on my part. After we had visited for a while, he asked if he could pray for me and I readily agreed. His prayer was filled with rich images and hopeful expressions for my recovery from COVID. I knew I had been prayed into God's care. When the prayer was over, he snapped a selfie of us on his cell phone revealing my disheveled state at the time (see photo previous page).

Several months after my hospitalization, I wrote an email message to Bonaventure which further indicates how I felt about his visit:

I was so grateful for your kindness and the time you took to visit me. Your attention to me was very moving, as was your prayer with me. Thank you for caring about someone you didn't even know, and for the respect you showed me when I was in such a weakened condition . . . Your faithfulness and compassion were well displayed that evening, and I am grateful beyond words. It was enlightening to know a little bit about your story and how you came to appear at my bedside.

After Bonaventure departed, the room was suddenly quiet and still. He was such an uplifting presence, expressing much needed support on the cusp of my hospital discharge. In the wake of his angelic visitation, I found myself pondering, with renewed amazement, at the connections in my life that would send a complete stranger with such a deep spirit to my bedside.

While trying to make email contact with Bonaventure, I communicated with his mother, Ann Quilter. She noted that "Kaiser Fontana had close to four hundred COVID patients, the most of any in our area." She also affirmed my conviction that "our nurses have been the beacon of hope (literally) for so many struggling against this scourge of death and destruction." Ann can be duly proud of Bonaventure for his commitment to his patients. With Ann's help, I sent my blog to Bonaventure and invited her to read it as well. In response she said, "I will preserve this for Bona's children and grandchildren."

Summary of Hospital Stay

Confined in a hospital room, tethered to an oxygen supply, weak with a contagious virus, I found myself vacillating among the things I could do. Sometimes the tedium was so prevalent I would try to fall asleep, resting just to pass the time. At other times I was too wide awake and gave myself little jobs to do—tidy my bed, collect my trash, take an inventory of my personal possessions. Once I had started the blog writing, I thought about what to write, and when I had the energy and the supplies I wrote. In some cases I mulled over the words to accurately describe my experience; other times the words came more spontaneously. Part of every hour was spent in some form of self-analysis, assessing my condition. Was I tired, bored, or hungry?

Today, from a reflective distance, there were strong touchstone moments that redeem the whole hospital experience. Setting aside the wonder of medicine and the compassionate care, which I do not discount in the least, I think of four specific things that kept me going through this ordeal.

From the early part of my hospitalization I think of Ben, the nurse who took charge of the patients in the Noodle. He brought hope and encouragement to people who were suffering. Ben's organization and care continues to impress me after nearly a year.

During the middle part of my stay in Kaiser, J.T.'s phone call did for me what I could not do for myself and what I had done for others. A pastor's prayer can seem like an expected part of the job for some people. Although I cannot recall a single word he prayed, his effort and thoughtfulness touched me deeply.

Bonaventure's visit, on my last night in the hospital, was a blessing that was both comforting and sacred in its scope. He was not required to be at my bedside, and he did not have to extend himself to meet a stranger, let alone one who was barely recovering from COVID. But his open and generous spirit made sure that I was enveloped with expressions of faith.

It may seem simplistic, but the window in my hospital room was also a gift to me. It was a lifeline of imagination and a pool of memory for my weary soul. If only for brief moments of time, I could sense a world beyond my present limits. These particular moments stand out to me as the means of grace that refilled my depleted well of faith.

6

The Long, Slow Recovery

"YOU CAN GO HOME tomorrow." Dr. Elghoul gave me that good news on Monday, December 28. I was feeling better, my supplemental oxygen intake had been reduced, and I had received two courses of Remdesivir. I was ready to put this whole experience in the rearview mirror. By phone, Sue and I discussed the logistics and made a tentative plan for getting me home with the help of Mary and Terry, my sister and brother-in-law.

Right on time—6:30 am—the lab tech entered my room to draw blood. "Even on the day I'm leaving?" I asked incredulously. She answered my complaint with some form of "Yes, they need to know how well you are as you leave." More of the daily hospital procedures unfolded, and for the record, these are the last filed vital signs at the end of my hospital encounter, taken at 8:07 am:

Blood Pressure	104/68
Pulse	74
Temperature	96.3
Oxygen Saturation	95%
Respiratory Rate	18

The "acute hypoxemic respiratory failure" I checked in with had been brought under control with the miracle of modern medicine and the "Specialty Care Team" that ministered to me with their medical expertise.

Even before breakfast arrived, Dr. Elghoul popped in to confirm that I was going to be released. Then he added, "Go home to finish recovering." Those few words spoke volumes! I was not completely healed but had recuperation time ahead of me. Everyone who came in to see me had a cheerful attitude as they echoed the doctor's news, some version of "You get to go home today!" The positivity was encouraging, and I smiled as broadly as I could each time I heard the welcome news. The man who had been my nurse said he was happy I was leaving. In an instant I knew what he meant, and he affirmed what I had presumed. He had seen so many people die of COVID and be wheeled out feet first—enough to last a lifetime. He was happy for me to be leaving very much alive, and so was I.

I don't remember how many calls we exchanged, but Sue and I began to make more detailed plans for my departure. Experience had taught me that being discharged from the hospital does not happen swiftly. I had seen that again when it took four or five hours for my first roommate, Alfredo, to depart. There are so many last-minute details needing attention before leaving. There were discharge orders to be filed, take- home medications for the pharmacy to fill, and after-care instructions to be delivered. An oxygen tank had to be secured to get me from the room to the car.

My Case Management Discharge Notes are informative, indicating that my transportation home was secured and that I would travel in PPE (masked). The record shows that my nutritional needs would be met and that I would have a responsible caregiver (Sue). I would be independent with home mobility but remain semi-dependent on my family. I would be supplied with durable medical equipment (oxygen). The discharge notes also show that my family is "in agreement with and aware of my discharge and post-hospitalization plans." Furthermore, I was to be in self-isolation as prescribed for two weeks, and I would be placed in the COVID Monitoring Program (CMP). With that, my Case Management handoff was completed.

All of these things were in motion. While they were being sorted, I calmly and purposefully organized my belongings, got myself cleaned up and dressed, and waited patiently as time passed. I wrote my final blog and worked a couple of crossword puzzles to help occupy my mind. I gazed through the glass of my friend the window at the world I would soon be re-entering. There were aspects of my stay I was not going to miss, but I felt a sense of deep gratitude for the professional care I had received.

A couple more phone calls were required to nail down the time for me to be picked up. Sue arranged for Mary and Terry to collect her, along with a tank of oxygen Apria had delivered, and come to Fontana to get me. They would pull into the circular drive in front of the hospital, let security know that they were there, and I would be released.

The sobering reflection that there were patients who would not be going home that day tempered my joy and anticipation of going home. They needed the acute care the hospital and its staff was providing—more oxygen, more medicine. As long as patients kept arriving and there was need for the War Zone, what I had gone through was being repeated with other souls. Some would be given even more critical care than I had received, like a ventilator, and for others it would be too late. As eager as I was to leave Room 708-B, any euphoria was softened by my awareness of the ongoing crisis.

When word came that they were ready for me, I got into a wheelchair and was attached to an oxygen tank. Before I was wheeled out the door I said to José, "*Vaya con Dios, mi amigo*" in my best Spanish. In reply he said, "Pray for me, Padre." As I passed the nurses' station, the staff said their cheerful goodbyes and I called out, "Thank you so much!" Before long, I was in the elevator descending to the ground floor. Coming out of the elevator and into the glass-walled corridor, the sun was almost too bright for my eyes. A few seconds later I was outdoors for the first time in two weeks, nearing the curb and searching for my family.

In the flurry of the next few minutes, I gave Terry my keys and told him where he could find my car in the nearby parking structure. He would be driving my car home. We decided where I would sit in Mary's car, how to arrange my oxygen tubing, and where the oxygen tank brought from home would be placed. For a minute or two, while others were handling these details, Sue and I had a few moments to embrace. It was wonderful to see each other, and tears of relief overcame us. The moment was fleeting but ever so sweet and memorable.

On the ride home I directed Mary, making it easier for her to navigate the route. It was a clear, bright day with a fresh layer of snow on the nearby mountains. As we passed them by, I looked at the landmarks I had seen from my hospital window, feeling a new sense of appreciation. After nearly two weeks in room 708-B, going home was surreal. Every nuance of the 18-mile journey seemed amplified. As I expressed my appreciation for Mary and Terry's help, I noted how we were a close family when we were younger, and how again we were relying on our family ties in this time of need.

There is a phenomenon in which something feels both strange and familiar at the same time. I had that feeling coming home. All that I had been through in the previous two weeks had been an ordeal, a crucible, and it felt peculiar to be beyond the constraints of Room 708-B. I was still feeling weak, especially with the physical movements and emotions of the last few hours. My biggest limitation was being tethered to the cannula at my nose and the clear ¼ inch tubing leading to the oxygen tank. For the next few weeks, oxygen tubing would be underfoot, threatening to trip us, medical devices could be found in several places around the house, and notes on slips of paper littered many flat surfaces.

Once inside the house, I walked over to sit in my dining room chair and simply looked around. Our dog, Dollie, came to welcome me home by jumping up on my lap. It was so good to see her. She didn't stay on my lap too long; there were too many people in the room and too much activity for her to settle for any length of time. Besides, Sue wanted me to check out the oxygen concentrator Apria had delivered and test out the seventy-five feet of tubing attached to it. We wanted to make sure the converter was positioned correctly and operating properly, and that the tubing would reach wherever I needed to go.

Once I safely transferred to the converter, we stored the oxygen tank in the garage in case we ever needed it to transport me outside the house. We also tested the adapter Apria provided for my C-PAP machine, learning how to connect my tubing to the oxygen converter during sleep. With these little hurdles crossed, Mary and Terry prepared to leave amid our heartfelt expressions of gratitude for their assistance in getting me settled. With their departure, I recall having a snack of peanut butter on half an English muffin, while I sorted through the piled up mail set aside for me. I don't recall any overly important communication with the exception of a slew of get well cards.

In the winter, daylight fades in the late afternoon. I watched a half hour of TV while Sue made some "we got him home" phone calls. On Facebook she posted this simple message: "Update: George is home!" I may have had a Lean Cuisine entrée for dinner, about the same size meal I had in the hospital. After that, my energy was flagging and I was ready to go to bed—in my own bed at last! It didn't take long before I was asleep, secure in the safety of my own bedroom, the oxygen converter softly humming, its dial light giving a soft blue glow to the room.

December 30

I woke up about 6:00 am, after about nine hours of mostly restful sleep while attached to my C-PAP. It was the penultimate day of 2020, the "CO-VID year." As quietly as I could, I started to stir, sitting up on the edge of the bed. Sue, ever alert and ready to help me if needed, was at my bedside as quickly as she could move. Once dressed in some lounge pants, a long sleeved shirt, and slippers, I slowly walked myself to the dining room and sat down. For the moment, which was all the energy I had. The oxygen converter had been set at three, so I was receiving 3 L/min. as I sat there letting the fog in my mind clear.

In a few minutes I began a series of small activities that would soon become routine. With Sue's careful monitoring, I took my temperature and used the pulse oximeter to measure my oxygen intake and heartbeat levels while Sue made note of the readings. These measurements would be repeated each day going forward in my recovery. What a pleasure it was to do these simple things at home, on my own schedule, rather than the hospital's 6:30 am routine.

Trying to replicate what I had received in the hospital, Sue provided me with a small bowl of cereal, a serving of canned peach chunks, half an English muffin, apple juice and tea, which she had purchased while I was still in the hospital. What a profound gift that we so often take for granted—the love and care of our spouses.

After breakfast, which Sue lovingly prepared for her weakened husband, I wanted to take a shower. This meant we had to work out how I would do this while I was attached to the oxygen tubing. The water would not be a problem for the plastic, but positioning the tubing was a challenge. Its weight kept pulling the tubing outside the shower door until I anchored it with a wet washcloth with enough tubing inside the shower door to achieve the task. I don't consider these little things until I have to think them through by necessity.

Following my shower, which was carefully monitored by Sue, I slipped into comfy clothes and began to read the backlog of newspapers delivered in my absence. A stack of dated newspapers is simply old news and it did not take me long. I quickly scanned the headlines and recalled the stories I had seen on TV in the hospital. The regular features I read each day drew my interest and I saved the crossword puzzles to solve later. It would be another day or two before I began to read email messages or make phone calls. One exception was to chime in on a call to wish my sister-in-law Jamie a happy birthday.

When I left the hospital I needed to inject myself with Lovenox for ten days to prevent blood clots from forming. I had given myself such injections before, so this was an easy thing to do. In addition, I was advised to take zinc sulfate, vitamin C and vitamin D as part of my recovery regimen.

ໟ

Kaiser's wonderful follow-up system, the COVID Monitoring Program (CMP), was efficient and thorough. I would be receiving a phone call from a nurse each day. Like clockwork, the call came on that first day home, and I was chatting with Sonata, a nurse with a most pleasant demeanor. I responded to questions about the oxygen converter setting and my pulse oximeter numbers. She reviewed my aftercare instructions, making sure that I was aware of every nuance. We spent a few minutes establishing what information would be needed in future follow-up calls. I was to be ready to make a report, but I was also free to ask any question I wanted about my care. Sonata also advised me that I would receive a phone call from a doctor the following day.

With me safely at home and able to fend for myself in a limited way, Sue planned to return to her volunteer work with RCRC/TM. I assured her I would be okay without her for a couple of hours. It would be fortuitous if she did go because she could bring me a taco for my lunch. I don't know if the COVID symptoms dimmed my taste buds or the fifteen hundred-calorie diabetic diet did the job, but I was craving something with some flavor, maybe a little spice for my palate.

December 31

New Year's Eve began at 8:25 am with a phone call from Dr. Imperio, as promised by Sonata. At his request, I reported that I was feeling a little better and my oxygen saturation was 93 percent with the concentrator set at 3 L/min. I had an occasional cough but had no shortness of breath. When Dr. Imperio asked if I was missing any outpatient medications, I answered no. The doctor's notes also revealed my diagnosis: Coronavirus COVID-19 pneumonia, but I knew that. His recovery advice was to keep "slowly improving" and continue with my present treatment. The entire phone call lasted ten minutes.

The new year would be upon us in a few hours. With little energy to do much of anything, I thought about how I had lost the Christmas season. It's funny how Christmas is a date on the calendar that is preceded by a series of expectations. In our culture we have any number of activities to help us prepare, such as ballets, plays, and all kinds of concerts. There's no end to the holiday-themed television shows and movies that are practically required watching each year. People plan their shopping, decorating and baking to fit into frenetic schedules. For some, Christmas is not complete without . . . (fill in the blank).

All of that disappeared this year when my health crisis left me with no energy to function and landed me in the hospital. I usually rely on the season of Advent to prepare room in my heart to celebrate the birth of Jesus. Those Advent wheels had barely started to turn when I became sick and couldn't worry about much of anything else. Now that I was at home, some of what I had missed came to mind.

The pandemic curtailed traditional happenings, or they became of necessity virtual events. For seven years I have sung in the Christmas programs of the Community Chorus of Redlands, but our rehearsals had been cancelled in March and the holiday concerts scrubbed. Christmas worship would be a Zoom or YouTube offering. The coronavirus protocols muted the seasonal decorations, parties, shopping and so much more. All of these events evaporated from my calendar and my mind until this reflective moment.

January 1

Christmas itself had come and gone while I was in the hospital, so we planned to celebrate on January 1. The festive Christmas tree was still on display in our living room with multiple presents wrapped beneath its branches, ready for giving. Matt came over and we opened our stockings and exchanged gifts. It didn't matter that we were a week beyond the actual holiday.

It was a joy to be alive to participate in our traditions. One gift I bought for Sue before my hospitalization had remained in the trunk of my car for three weeks. It never got wrapped and was still in the store's bag when Matt went to fetch it for me. Other gifts had been bought through Amazon and delivered while I was laid up, with one gift back-ordered and due to arrive on January 4. Our celebration was as good as any other year, but the reason for our delayed observance was never far from my mind.

Sue wrote a New Year's Day post on Facebook with this sincere message: "Thank you all for your prayers for George. He is making slow, but steady progress. I'm so grateful to have him home." Both of us were feeling the blessings of starting a new year with an eye to better health in the future.

> **COVID TRACKING—January 2021**
> **Cases: 19,346,790 / Deaths: 356,783**

In the first two weeks of 2021, I would extend myself a little more each day while staying attuned to how I felt. Somedays I would feel strong in the morning but my energy would flag by lunchtime. I kept my mind active as I passed through the day, which I knew would help me sleep better at night. I didn't want to relapse, but I was alert and able to function in a limited way, ever aware of my breathing and oxygen saturation percentage. I surprised my Lectionary Study Group colleagues by Zooming in on January 5 to lead the discussion of a lesson I had prepared weeks earlier. They had a lot of questions for me, and I did my best to answer before my exertion got the better of me. It felt especially good to be in contact with my friends, wonderful to see their faces, and I would join them each week thereafter.

Two unexpected things happened to my body that first full week of January. First, I developed a rash on my feet, thighs and groin. It was quite itchy and red, almost like the measles. I couldn't tell if this was some lingering effect of the coronavirus or something more sinister. Rather than be anxious about the rash, I decided it must be something benign, perhaps some type of contact dermatitis. I asked Sue to buy me some calamine lotion, and that helped some. But the rash quickly spread to my stomach, back and armpits and I needed something more. I took pictures and sent them to the CMP team. I suppose the rash was some kind of humorous irony. I had survived a life-threatening virus and now I was itching like crazy!

I had a post-hospitalization telephone follow-up call with my primary care physician and brought the rash to his attention. He prescribed an antibiotic; however, the rash had diminished significantly before the prescription was filled.

The other unexpected thing had to do with my nasal passages, which was worrisome for me as I was trying to breathe. It seemed that the oxygen being delivered through a cannula into my nose was drying me up considerably. Overnight and in the morning, but also all through the day, my sinuses were producing large, bloody clots of mucus which were difficult to express.

The first suggested remedy came from Sue: use some nasal saline spray. The CMP nurses heartily endorsed this idea. However, as the problem persisted, they mentioned an over-the-counter product, Ayr saline nasal gel. I had never heard of it, but Sue bought some for me, and the breathing relief it offered in combination with the nasal saline spray did the trick.

Many people had found a way to communicate with Sue once they learned I was in the hospital. Some reached out to her through Facebook, offering her comfort and support. Others touched base with her via email, saying they were praying for both of us in this trying time. A few surprised her with a phone call, and she provided an update when someone called. Sue was most grateful for the well-wishes that came her way. I would learn about the callers during our daily conversations.

While I was recovering, and when I felt up to it, I placed a few calls of my own to express my gratitude. I strongly felt the need to touch base those who had shown their concern for me during this crisis. Beyond "thank you," I wasn't sure what the words would be. How could I say what their interest in and love for me had meant? I know I was deeply appreciative of their phone calls and messages. Surely my words would be inadequate.

One of the first calls was to my college roommate, Jerry McBride. I had last spoken with him in a video call a few days before becoming ill. I wanted him to know that I was out of danger and now recovering at home. We chatted a few minutes before he could sense my energy fading.

A call with my friend Gilbert Stones was much the same. He suggested that I would probably write a song about my experience, and I told him that was not going to happen. Gilbert knows well that I often express my experiences and emotions through songwriting, but somehow this illness had drained my creative energy. This experience was too personal to reflect it in a song. Even months after my recovery I find no reason to "celebrate" this disease through poetry or lyrics. I still can't think of how I would express my sadness for those who had suffered and died, my appreciation for those who had cared for me, and my delight in being alive. Gilbert could also sense when my strength was flagging, and he politely limited our call.

One day I surprised my District Superintendent, Melissa McKinnon (who had called Sue on December 20) to thank her for her concern and prayers. She said that no one had ever returned a call to her with such an expression of appreciation. Two friends of long standing, Rex and Bonnie, had also talked with Sue, and I called to let them know how much it meant to me that they reached out to her to ask after me.

Earlier in our lives, my siblings and I were part of close-knit family, depending on each other as we moved around as a military family. We have always been in contact with each other through the years, aware of the changes we were going through and sensitive to each other's physical and emotional experiences in our lives. We all have developed distinct personalities and filtered our common history through our individual lenses.

Our older sister, Sharon, lived in Ohio for many years and was not in close proximity to the rest of us, though she was included in major events; we stayed in contact with her through phone calls and occasional visits. Sharon died more than a decade ago, but we still remember how she was an integral part of our lives.

Our youngest sibling, brother John, has lived in Nevada for nearly forty years now. As the "baby" of the family he has sometimes been on the short side of our collective experiences. He was a bit rebellious in his teens but has become a solid family man. Since he lives out of state, we touch base with John by phone on birthdays and holidays. If we travel his way, we stop for a brief visit, maybe a dinner together, and do our catching up.

The phone call I made to my brother John touched me the most deeply. After I brought him up to date on my recovery process he said something I will never forget. Through tear-filled emotion, John said, "I prayed that God would take me and let you live. You are a much better man than me." I can still hear his voice breaking as he spoke those words. I told John how much those words meant to me, but I offered my reassurance that I was glad we both had lived through this pandemic. I know he has a lot to offer this world and his big family, and I didn't deserve his loving words. I am deeply sad that John died in February of 2022, and I did not have the chance to talk with him further about his feelings.

The love and concern we have for each other is an emotional bond I treasure, especially as I age. My siblings' attention and worry for me during my illness, and their helpfulness in meeting my needs, is a gift that I can never repay. One lesson I've learned through this is how important family connections continue to be. I am grateful for the loving foundation our parents instilled in us and that developed among us as we were growing up together.

I made numerous other phone calls and answered dozens of email messages during the initial stages of my recovery. Most of the calls lasted a few minutes, but a few people wanted to know more about my experience and asked me questions about having had COVID-19. Two questions stick with me: While you were in the hospital were you ever afraid of dying? My answer is that the whole experience was frightening, but I felt like I was receiving loving care and trusted that I would get better. Did you wonder about where God was for you? The short answer is no, but my lowest point was hitting the wall where I couldn't pray. It's not that God wasn't there for me. It was my inability to sense God's presence because of my illness.

⚭

Like so many people, the events of January 6 horrified me. The insurrection at the U.S. Capitol, where a dangerous mob attacked Congress in a futile attempt to stop the certification of the presidential election, seemed utterly pointless. It was clear who was instigating this lawlessness and sad to see that people lost their lives over one politician's big lie. I was glad to see that the House and Senate completed their Constitutional work despite the rebellion of that day. Two weeks later, I celebrated the inauguration of a new president and vice president and the beginning of a new administration. It felt like a breath of fresh air, a metaphor that now had new meaning to me.

⚭

On the January 7 phone call, the nurse I spoke with encouraged me to adjust the oxygen flow settings from the concentrator, testing to see if I could sustain a 93 percent or more oxygen saturation. Adjustments could be made up or down depending on the oxygen saturation readings. If my level was holding steady at 97 percent, I could lower the setting by a half or a whole step; if I dropped below 93 percent I was supposed to bump up the setting. It was a trial and error process, and I was to monitor how I felt with each adjustment.

My strength was growing when in the following week (January 13), I rejoined my siblings of the California-Pacific Chapter of the Order of Saint Luke for Evening Prayer. Being unable to sing even a few notes or read aloud more than half a sentence, I opted to be a listener rather than lead any element of the service. With mild January days on tap, I decided to try my hand at watercolor painting again (January 16) and produced an artwork I dubbed "Narrow Passage," likely a subconscious reference to the COVID crucible I had endured.

In mid-January, the weather is usually mild enough on Martin Luther King Jr. weekend that I can prune our rose bushes for the winter. I was fretting about how to do this while tethered to oxygen. Could I switch from the converter to the tank and keep receiving the oxygen upon which I was relying? I had already discovered that I could step outside without disconnecting my oxygen tubing. It may have been only a few feet, but I was outside in the fresh air and sunshine.

Before I was aware of what she was doing, Sue began to tackle the rose pruning job. When she asked for my guidance, I stepped outside to help. I discovered I could go further if I went through the garage, so I got a little closer to where she was working and could talk with her instead of shouting from a distance. Sue had intended to work on two or three roses, but before the end of the weekend she had pruned all seventeen of our rosebushes. It was not a task she wanted to do, but with my limitations she completed the job like a champion. Here was yet another way she was showing her love and support for me.

Years of preaching have attuned me to the rich images and metaphors found in Scripture, and yet I often fail to link those ideas with my own life right away. Some time may pass before hindsight helps me see how to apply what I experience to a scriptural story. As I look back on watching Sue, I think of Jesus' teachings about pruning (John 15:1–8) or the song of the vineyard (Isa 5:1–7) and wonder if they apply to my COVID encounter.

What was taken away from me to allow for new growth? Will my "roots" grow stronger and lead to some kind of fruitful abundance? Has COVID been a season of pruning in my life? Clearer answers may come in time, but for now maybe the virus' effects had humbled some unproductive part of my life. At this point, I am more inclined to think about a roses and thorns analogy. COVID has certainly been a thorn to me, so life on this side of recovery must be the roses. I certainly accept both the blessings and the challenges that come along.

For the first six weeks of my recovery I would receive regular phone calls from the CMP nurses. The calls came at various times of the day, and the information they requested was always the same. Whether it was Sonata, Terri, Armando, Quiana or someone else, they wanted to know my temperature reading, my oxygen saturation and my pulse rate. I have records of that data for January 2 through February 8. Each day has between four and nine entries, depending on my faithfulness in making notes.

Here is a sample:

Date	Time	O$_2$	Pulse	Temp	Conv[1]
1/7	6:30 am	93	80	96.9	3
	9:00 am	97	58		
	11:30 am	93	61		
	1:07 pm	97	82		
	3:30 pm	93	87		2.5
	4:50 pm			96.1	
	7:30 pm	97	87		

Around this time (mid-January), I started feeling better, and I decided I was not going to be sick anymore. It was more a mental frame of mind than a physical one. I shed the loungewear and slippers and started dressing in pants and a shirt. I put on socks and shoes and began to exhibit more strength.

The CMP nurses encouraged me to ask questions and I regularly had four or five ready when they called. Along with my statistical reports, I would report what physical problems I had experienced the previous day. Most of my problems were minor and I described what I had done for relief.

Once, I told the nurse that my legs were swollen, and they said to try walking for increasing lengths of time, five, ten, maybe fifteen minutes, depending on my energy and breathing levels. Another idea the nurses offered was to try some lung exercises. Per their recommendation, I downloaded a set of breathing exercises from Johns Hopkins Medicine and began to add those practices to my daily routine.

During these days of my recovery, I was mindful of not stressing myself physically, but that also led to a sense of how dull my routine was becoming. To relieve any feeling of boredom, I assigned myself little tasks that I could accomplish without too much effort—tidying my desk, writing a note, or any computer-oriented task. I returned to the Sunday afternoon and Wednesday evening prayer Zoom calls with my OSL friends and when the house was quiet began to add moments of meditation to my daily routine. I began to read some of the books I received as Christmas presents. Anything I attempted did not push me beyond my physical limits.

Weaning Off Oxygen

When Sharon became my CMP nurse on January 25, the daily visits changed to weekly exchanges, and with her my questions changed. I was no longer focused on my physical ailments but looking toward my post-recovery future. I asked, "Am I still contagious?" She said, "No," because of the antibodies in my system after having COVID pneumonia. I wondered, "Can I be reinfected?" Yes, under certain circumstances such as new variants that crop up. With vaccines so prominent in the news I asked, "When can I get vaccinated?" Sharon said it would be 90 days after I left the hospital, so that would be no sooner than March 29. I inquired, "Why are my fingers so cold?" (I was having trouble getting a reading on the pulse oximeter with colder than usual fingers.) She said I could improve my circulation by becoming more active.

Sharon then made a big suggestion. She advised that the time had come for me to try weaning myself off the oxygen and advised me on a plan. For a couple of weeks I had been adjusting the level of oxygen I was receiving. My overnight settings were 3.0 or 3.5, but with good oxygen saturation numbers, I could reduce the settings to 2.5 or 2.0. I also made mid-day adjustments. For example, following a setting of 3.0 overnight, we dropped it to 2.5 after my morning shower. Later in the day I would drop it to 2.0 or raise it to 2.5 while maintaining a 96 percent to 98 percent saturation level. My temperature stayed in the 96.0° to 98.0° range, and my pulse rate was consistently in the mid- to upper 70s. It was time to stop using the oxygen for increasing lengths of time.

On January 26, following Sharon's instructions, I set aside the oxygen and bravely began the weaning process. I was nervous about going without the supplemental oxygen. Would I be able to breathe on my own? At first, to help with this anxiety, I planned low-level activities. To help myself be disciplined with the weaning, I created an "Oxygen Weaning Schedule" to chart my progress. It started with setting the converter at 2.0 for an hour, then setting it to 1.0 for the next hour. That pattern repeated throughout the waking hours of the day. The setting would be 2.5 overnight. The next day I would use a setting of 2.0 for one hour, then reduce it to 1.0 for the next two hours, and that pattern continued throughout the day. I was to listen to my body, adjusting the converter up or down accordingly, and I became more comfortable without the added oxygen.

On the third day, the pattern changed. I set the converter at 1.0 for the morning hours, I then raised it to 2.0 for an hour, then lowered to 1.0 for the next four hours. I was using less oxygen and maintaining good oxygen saturation. The fourth day would be a big test. I started with a 1.0 setting of the converter for one hour and then turned it off for the next hour. Every other hour throughout the day I was off the oxygen and breathing well on my own. My lowest oxygen level was 92 percent, but regularly hovered at an average of 97 percent—perfectly normal.

The weaning process was working! Even with less supplemental oxygen my strength was returning. A real turning point was when I forgot to turn on the converter ninety minutes after I should have. I was becoming more active and involved with life beyond the tether. As a Zoom event, I resumed meeting with the Redlands Fortnightly Club. Founded on January 24, 1895, it is the second oldest literary club in the United States. I became a member in 2015. The club gathers fortnightly to present papers that have been researched and written by its members. I was glad for the opportunity to be involved with the club again, and to see my fellow members on the screen after several months of the club's pandemic-related inactivity.

During January, Sue and I learned of the December 13 death of our tax consultant of 34 years. Richard had been a kidney transplant recipient two decades or more ago, but he was diagnosed with colon cancer and struggled with chemotherapy and immunotherapy treatments through the year until his weakened body gave out. An upbeat memorial service for him took place, which I watched via a YouTube live stream. For me, Richard's death was a stark reminder of human mortality, especially in the light of my all-too-recent brush with death.

The last Saturday in January I was feeling well enough to try my hand at driving. I had been home for a month, my strength and stamina were growing, and I was both eager and anxious to leave the house. I felt I needed to end my recovery self-isolation. I also realized it had been six weeks since I had filled up my car's gas tank. I devised a simple plan. I would drive to the nearby gas station to refuel and then to a Subway sandwich shop for lunch. I could do this while I was off the oxygen converter in keeping with my weaning schedule.

Sue, naturally, was nervous but agreed to go with me in case I had a problem. Filling up the gas tank was the easy part, and I was finished in ten minutes. The sub shop was next. It didn't appear too busy when I arrived but a patron ahead of me placed a large multi-sandwich order. It was taking so long that Sue got out of the car, worried about my whereabouts, only to find me patiently waiting to order. A few more minutes passed before I completed my purchase and we were headed home. Sue was concerned, but I was none the worse for wear, and I had driven all of two miles. This was another sign of my recovery progress.

The days of January seemed to crawl by slowly, and I was discovering how COVID-19 had affected me. For one thing, I had lost twenty-two pounds while in the hospital, most likely due to the strict diet I was given. When the month began, my body was weak and listless, and my mind felt like it was in slow motion. I was experiencing physical maladies I'd never seen before. A lot was happening to me and I felt the loss of control that goes with being a patient. That's why in mid-January I knew I wanted to stop being sick. It was a turning point in my recovery but not an immediate change of trajectory. There would be many good days ahead, but some days the limits of my physical condition were evident.

January melted into February and the pace of my life gently increased. I was stronger and more capable of tending to my own needs, simple things like folding laundry, making meals and washing dishes. Once I shed the restraints of the oxygen tubing, I tried my hand at raking a small collection of leaves or other light yard work. Life for me was gradually advancing to a pre-COVID-19 state, but the impressions of the disease were firmly planted in my mind and spirit.

About once an hour I paused to take a deep, cleansing breath. That helped me pay attention to my breathing and reminded me of how challenging it was to sustain my breath, even while receiving supplemental oxygen. Each time my strength was waning, I recalled lying in that hospital bed. With every shower I was realizing the joy of bathing myself, grateful I didn't have to wait for help. As I was able to prepare my own meals, I was thankful for those who brought me trays of food each day. These simple quotidian things became more meaningful to me with each passing day.

> **COVID TRACKING—February 2021**
> **Cases: 25,817,939 / Deaths: 455,613**

The better I felt the more I wanted to know different things. On our February 1 telephone visit, I asked nurse Sharon, "Should I continue weaning?" Her simple answer was yes. "Should I stop using the oxygen?" Yes, for increasing lengths of time, and according to how you feel. "Listen to your body," she advised. Then I asked my big question, "When could I be cleared for work?" Sharon said there was no magic formula and this question is answered on a case by case basis. It was disheartening to hear but Sharon said the number of days in the hospital would equal the number of weeks it takes to recover. I had been in the hospital for fourteen days and, feeling as good as I was feeling, I could not imagine recovery taking fourteen weeks. At that point I was only five weeks into my recovery.

Looking at my Kaiser medical records, and Sharon's notes for our February 1 conversation, I find some interesting items. I had not had a fever for the past three days and taken no fever-reducing medication. My coughs and shortness of breath had decreased. I was speaking in full sentences without audible wheezes or signs of distress. Sharon advised me to avoid overexertion and have rest periods throughout the day. I was to use a saltwater gargle two to three times a day, and drink plenty of water (and Gatorade) each day. I never drank so much Gatorade in all of my life before this!

I had my last conversation with Sharon on February 8, and we discussed my returning to normal activities and possibly going back to work. Really, I had two questions, "Could my forgetfulness be due to COVID?" Her answer was, "It could be; it varies by individual cases." I reported to Sharon that I had not used any oxygen since February 4—four days—and I was breathing on my own while maintaining a 97 percent oxygen saturation level. This led to a discussion about driving to Hemet, 30 miles away, for a tax appointment. Her reply, "Yes, if you're feeling up to it." I was.

I spent part of my recovery preparing to meet a new tax consultant. I was thinking about combining a trip to the Trinity Lutheran Church office with my tax appointment but decided that my tax appointment would be enough of a challenge for my first big outing. As a precaution, I brought along an oxygen tank in case I felt the need. The trip and the tax appointment on February 10 both were uneventful. I did make another trip to Hemet ten days later for a church leaders' planning meeting, all part of how I was making my way back to work.

Not everything about January and February is crystal clear in my memory. I made a lot of notes about my recovery progress, but there are some mundane things that are a blur. I wrote thank you notes but I can't recall everyone I sent them to. There are gaps in my Oxygen Weaning Chart where I was either too distracted or indifferent to make notations. I received many get well cards but set them aside to review later. I don't remember every phone call I had, but what I remember is the feeling of being loved and cared for in my time of weakness. This made me appreciate the people who thought about me and took the time to express their concern.

Throughout this time, I gradually began to feel human again. For a few minutes each day, I'd play something on my guitar, picking out a familiar melody without trying to sing. I often read at night as I go to bd, and with a backlog of magazines to read there was no shortage of material. My usual practice of praying the Daily Office resumed (most days) as I found the stamina to focus my prayer concerns. In weaker moments I'd plop down on the couch and watch a recorded TV program. Returning each of these activities to my daily living helped me pass my recovery time and contributed to my return to a sense of normalcy. I was becoming more myself.

As far as going back to work was concerned, Sharon's advice was that I could give it a try as long as I had no fever for at least ten days. The highest fever I recorded during my recovery was 99.1°. She added that I did not have to be retested for COVID in order to return to work. I knew that everyone coming to the church office would be masked and social-distanced. At the time, we were pre-recording elements of the service, including the sermon, so the risks would be relatively low. I determined to give it a try and see if I had the stamina to work. My first Sunday back was February 21, the first Sunday in Lent.

While I may not have been technically "cured" of my COVID disease experience, I was well on my way to recovery. When people asked, I would answer that I was feeling 95 percent better, listening to my body and trying not to exert myself beyond what I could safely tolerate. With the exception of a trip to Hemet for the start of a Lenten Bible study, most of my activities were limited to Zoom meetings (including the Bible study) and I stayed at home every day. The worst of what I had experienced was behind me, but I was attentive to my energy levels so I could avoid any hint of a relapse. I would never want to go through that again.

> **COVID TRACKING—March 2021**
> **Cases: 28,244,591 / Deaths: 521,837**

When the month of March arrived my activity level increased, but the events on my calendar show that Zoom gatherings remained prominent. Still, some notable happenings took place. On March 4, I drove Sue and Matt to the Living Desert Zoo and Gardens in Palm Desert, to have an adventure and to celebrate my seventieth birthday. It was a lovely day, and I was glad to have the stamina to walk around without difficulty. We scheduled a gate repair and fence replacement job after a four month delay. A long-overdue oil change for my car led to a series of other auto maintenance jobs. Taking care of these simple things became satisfying achievements. Sue had hand surgery on St. Patrick's Day and I helped her spend the next two weeks trying to keep the bandages clean and dry.

Nurse Sharon had ordered a bone density test for me, but I was unaware of this until I was told that the appointment had been booked. The following day, after fifteen months of no dental care, I had an appointment with a new dentist. What a relief to have my teeth cleaned and to hear the report that I needed no follow up dental work. Near the end of the month, my niece Patty and her sons came from Ohio to Southern California for a visit, and we had dinner with my sisters and their husbands at a local Mexican restaurant. It was fun to have such a meaningful outing, doing such a normal thing post-COVID.

What I had looked forward to eagerly happened at the end of the month—getting vaccinated. A virus like COVID does not go away. I waited the full 90 days after my hospitalization and made my vaccine appointment for March 30. Kaiser Permanente handled the process with its usual efficiency.

I checked in at the clinic, filled out some paperwork, and waited my turn. When called, I walked in and sat down at the table where I had been led. A few questions later, the needle was in my arm and I received the first dose of the Moderna vaccine. This seemed like a giant step in my recovery, and I felt both grateful and relieved to be immunized. As directed, I moved to a waiting area where I would pass the next fifteen minutes to make sure I did not have any adverse reaction to the shot. At the appropriate time, I picked up my vaccination card and I was on my way. My second Moderna vaccine would be administered on April 23, exactly four weeks after the first shot.

> **COVID TRACKING—April 2021**
> **Cases: 30,095,776 / Deaths: 553,934**
> **COVID TRACKING—May 2021**
> **Cases: 31,948,761 / Deaths: 574,601**
> **COVID TRACKING—June 2021**
> **Cases: 32,938,999 / Deaths: 591,392**

7

Lessons Learned

As I SAID IN the Introduction, this is a personal story, my story, about how I experienced COVID-19 and the world around it. With the very notable exceptions of two weeks in the hospital and six weeks of recovering at home, my life seemed very ordinary between March of 2020 and March of 2021. I don't take those two months of being sick for granted in any way. I feel blessed to be alive to write these words and grateful for all the attention sent my way in what was undoubtedly the worst season of my life.

My COVID Crucible was just that, a test of my health and strength, a challenge which affected my body and my spirit, a trial that has altered my perceptions and expectations. Whenever I see temporary shelters beside a hospital, I'll think of the War Room and the Noodle I experienced. I see the media reports of COVID cases and I vividly recall my time in the hospital. Every needle jab shown on TV reminds me of being ill and the steps we can take to minimize our risk. I would not wish this illness on anyone. I take from this experience a sense of wonder and gratitude that I have been graced with a loving wife, a supportive family, an extended community of friends, and a renewed appreciation for life itself. Thanks be to God!

I continue to feel gratitude for the love and support I have received through this crucible. I am grateful for the medical care given to me in many of my worst moments. That I remain "on this side of the grass," means more to me than ever before. To be able to breathe freely, continue in my career, treasure my family, and enjoy everyday life is a gift I appreciate every day. It is a privilege to have the means to write these thoughts, and I pray that others may learn something from my experience. If nothing else, we must never take our health for granted, especially in the face of a public health crisis like this.

COVID for me now feels like an experience in my rearview mirror. As each day passes and my health remains steady, the virus and its aftermath have become a part of my history. That does not mean I am complacent about the disease and the many people who have suffered because of it. I clearly recall the difficulty I had breathing and the elevated levels of oxygen required to sustain my life. I remember the weakness I felt and the treatments I received. The care given to me is etched in my mind. I will not forget the long hours in the hospital or recovering at home. Most of all, I do not want to be maudlin about my brush with COVID. I do not wish to wallow in self-pity for having been sick, nor use that experience as a crutch. I am glad to be a survivor, one who is a *recovery* statistic.

These days I think a lot about the number of people who turn their heads and act as if this whole public health crisis is somehow a hoax. Why is it that the politicizing of the virus sways so many people that they cannot accept common sense reasoning? Why are they so quick to criticize and so slow to participate in actions that will curb this disease? It puzzles me that people are so selfish that they can't help others, so set in their ways that they won't contribute to the efforts to stop, control or eradicate COVID-19 from our lives. You want to be finished with the coronavirus? Start being part of the solution!

On my less charitable days I think if someone refuses to wear a mask and rejects the idea of getting vaccinated, then they should be denied treatment or placed at the end of the line. When I wear my empathetic hat, I know that the Hippocratic Oath demands a compassionate response to those in need. Ultimately, I hope our nation has (or will) learn the lesson of our vulnerability in the face of this pathogen and our need to cooperate with our public health advisories.

I would not wish this disease on my worst critic, and I hope that everyone who suffers will be helped. I pray that medical personnel will be valued and given respite from their work. I hope that medical supplies will be abundant and available. Too many lives have been lost. Too much time, money and energy have been spent dealing with COVID in our society. Too many resources have been consumed and caregivers sorely tested. We cannot be cavalier about the toll this disease has taken on the social fabric and psyche of the world.

Ralph Waldo Emerson, the mid-nineteenth century American essayist, wrote, "This time like all times is a very good one, if we but know what to do with it." The prolonged era of the coronavirus pandemic has elevated this Emerson quote in my thinking, giving rise to numerous questions. What are the lessons we'll learn? How will we manage to survive and keep going? What challenges have we met during this trying time? Will we see any development of our character, either personally or collectively? What vulnerabilities have been exposed during this crisis, and what will we do about them? What good things have emerged because we have endured this era?

In a *Time* magazine issue dealing with the climate crisis, another major existential challenge of our time, Judith Butler, professor emeritus at the University of California at Berkeley wrote the following:

> *Pandemic* is etymologically *pan-demos*, all the people, or perhaps more precisely, the people everywhere. The "demos" is all the people despite the legal barriers that seek to separate them. A pandemic, then, links all the people through the potentials of infection and recovery, suffering and hope, immunity and fatality. No border stops the virus from traveling if humans travel; no social category secures absolute immunity for those it includes.[1]

Professor Butler reminds us how interconnected we are and how we affect each other's lives. But our shared world is not evenly shared. Some can easily access resources, others cannot cobble together life's basics—food, water, shelter, clothing, health care or economic security. Some folks have mounting unpayable debts while others live in such wealth they cannot fathom the struggles that come when such necessities are absent.

Author John Freeman writes about how dramatically COVID-19 shifted our gears. He noted,

> During the pandemic, businesses, governments and people made sudden severe changes to stay safe. People stayed indoors for weeks. Some for months. They didn't hug or shake hands. They wore masks. They worked a job and taught their children. Here was an immediate threat to life, and were it not for these drastic changes, scores more would have died.[2]

---

1. Butler, Judith, "Toward a Shared Space," 85.
2. Freeman, John, "New Narrative," 93.

Freeman says that we need a similar accelerated pace of change in dealing with the climate crisis or our world is likely to become uninhabitable very soon. My point in citing his essay is to say if people could make changes in the way we dealt with a public health crisis, rapidly or otherwise, we could find ways of promptly altering our social fabric to improve lives.

The COVID-19 pandemic laid bare a number of disparities in our society. Inequities in our health care system revealed racial divides, with a disproportional number of people of color affected by COVID. One can get lost in the "rabbit hole" of statistics, but one chart stood out for me. A Harvard report[3] noted these racial disparities in COVID-19 related deaths:

Race	Deaths/per 100,000	Race	Deaths/per 100,000
Black	118.8	Latinx	99.2
Indigenous	111.8	Asian	44.8
Pacific Islander	105.8	White	33.3

The report contained a non-exhaustive list of factors as reasons for this disparity:

- No access to testing
- Live in high density
- Be exposed to pollution
- Having a pre-existing condition
- Be an essential worker
- A racial bias in health care

This report shows how the economic landscape exposes the injustices of income inequality and how tentative life can be. Too many people live just one paycheck away from financial disaster.

Writers have put their metaphors to work trying to describe what the COVID experience has been for our world. One called it "a long period of collective hibernation," while another said we were "emerging from our dark isolation." As winter became spring in 2021, there was a growing sense of optimism about going back to some sense of pre-pandemic normal. A growing number of people were getting vaccinated and were venturing out to newly re-opened restaurants or other public places.

3. Li, "Racial Disparities in COVID-19."

However, all is not rosy. One author put it this way:

> [Post-pandemic] we are all a little traumatized. Psychiatrists have dubbed fear of returning to normal life "re-entry anxiety," and the American Psychological Association reports that about half of all Americans feel anxious about resuming in-person, indoor interactions.[4]

After working at home for months, some people were returning to workplaces, but with a measure of uncertainty. A columnist noted a variety of changes in the American workplace and the work/life balance:

> [People are] reassessing their relationship to their job . . . Millions of people have spent the last year re-evaluating their priorities.

The same article declared,

> The line between work and home has been blurring for decades— and with the pandemic, obliterated completely for many of us, as we have been literally living at work.[5]

Some people look for a "new normal" post-pandemic. I didn't care for the phrase "new normal" from the moment I first heard it. Things are either normal or new, not both. Some people seek ways we as a society can improve our interactions, a "way things could be" kind of viewpoint. Others look for a return to comfortable habits and routines, "the way things were" perspective. I believe each of us must wrestle with these challenging questions:

- Was COVID an inconvenient interruption?
- Was COVID an opportunity to apply ourselves to being better human beings?
- Was COVID a thing to be endured or a thing to be survived?

How we answer these questions will depend on our perceptions of life. The pandemic showed how kind and thoughtful people can be, but it also revealed how selfish and careless we are.

From my point of view, COVID offered us a chance to be innovative and creative, and experiment with new ways of relating to each other. We could practice our patience and understanding, take care of the environment (with fewer cars and planes polluting the world), and look for ways

---

4. Eliana Dockterman, "Ready to Commit?" 83.
5. Lipman, Joanne, "Pandemic Revealed How Much We Hate Our Jobs," 57–58.

to serve others. The pandemic gave families the opportunity to draw closer together and find better means of communication. Some people have used this time to break free from constraints and enter a new phase of their life. This was a time for me to trust God, seek the truth behind the public hyperbole, and work toward peace, love and hope in my relations with others.

As I write this, America is in the throes of reopening with relaxed COVID restrictions. Businesses are returning to pre-pandemic levels of operation, including workers returning to the office after working from home for a year or more. Restaurants are pretty much in full swing, with people dining out and socializing more. Sports venues, churches, libraries, and museums have opened to near capacity levels.

This reopening is possible because of the COVID vaccines. At the same time, there is hesitancy about the vaccines (for a variety of reasons), and new variants of the virus continue to plague the unvaccinated population. Valiant efforts have been made to educate the public and provide shots for the populace.

COVID-19 is still with us and will not go away because we want it to. This continues to be a public health crisis, and yet there are some who continue to treat the disease as a political issue. David French, a *Time* columnist, put his finger on it when he wrote,

> The history of the pandemic is intertwined with the culture war, and from the beginning, the response to COVID has broadly split between blue and red, urban and rural . . .

French points a finger at Donald Trump and the "blaze of disinformation that over time constructed the partisan alignment that followed. Red Americans disproportionately resisted COVID restrictions, while blue Americans largely embraced then."[6]

In many ways, this "year of COVID"—and I know it is lasting 18 months or more—has been a time of learning, listening, and looking for the best ways to respond. As foolish as some people have been, there have been very sensible voices who have guided us through this challenging era. This has called for us to be discerning and prudent in our trust of public officials. We each have had a role to play in addressing this disease. Our compliance with the guidelines and restrictions are not just a matter of "following the rules," but a matter of saving lives.

---

6. French, "Can We Escape the Vaccine Culture War," 28.

Others will be more sophisticated as they write about the world's experience with COVID-19. In fact, I have quoted some of the authors whose prose has meant something to me and given me an approach to this story I would not otherwise have had. My social commentary may not carry the weight of a journalist or a cultural critic. However, the illness I survived, the collective factors I have mentioned, and the attitudes I have noticed along the way, have given rise to my critique.

Two years ago I had never heard of COVID-19. Now I've learned more about it than I ever thought I would. This virus has been a distant concept, a challenge for the scientific community, an endless topic for the news, a physical reality in my life, and an ongoing fact of life for all of us. A multitude of questions remain, and it may take the remainder of my lifetime for answers to develop. Going forward, I will trust in the medical science that opens the doors to understanding this illness and listen to the advisors who guide our public response. I will weigh the information provided by our leaders and listen for the truth in their words. I will continue to act in ways that maximize the health and well-being of those around me. Most of all, I will treasure each day and taste the goodness of life as I live it.

Acknowledgements

THERE CAN NEVER BE enough words to express my gratitude to all the people who prayed for me while I was suffering from COVID pneumonia. Your concern for my welfare is a gift that warms my heart and humbles me.

Those who mailed get well cards and sent gifts to cheer me up in my distress . . . those who provided food for us during my recuperation . . . those who phoned to check on me, or paid me a visit, however brief or risky it may have been for you, added speed to my recovery.

I am grateful to the Rev. Andrew Welch for his interest in my story and his willingness to serve as my initial editor of this volume. His insights and invaluable suggestions have improved the contents of this volume and honored me with his time and attention.

It must not go without saying that the doctors, nurses, medical staff and hospital personnel who have given many extended hours of their time to treat COVID patients, have performed valuable service to hundreds of people, including this indebted author.

If you have given of yourself to help me through this experience and I have not mentioned you or recognized your contributions to my wellbeing, I ask your forgiveness and understanding.

The COVID Blog

| *Note: This is the blog that is the genesis of the book.*

| *Notes for these observations were written on paper towels and other scraps of paper that I could find near my hospital bed to write my reflections down as they occurred to me. No editing has been done to what I have written except to explain an incomplete thought or clarify a comment.*

<u>Blog Entry #1—Four Nurses</u>
December 18, 2020

The front line medical workers in the coronavirus pandemic have been rightly hailed as heroes for the dedicated work they do in caring for COVID patients. I became one of those patients on December 16 and witnessed first-hand the knowledge, skills and compassionate care the nurses provided in a challenging environment. With a ratio of six to one, the nursing staff was stretched thin and had to deal with multiple questions and requests for help from their patients. Here is a brief sketch of four of those nurses.

    <u>Randi</u>—At first she didn't tell me her name, and it took a while to determine that she was, in fact, an RN and just one of dozens helping with the massive triage happening around me. She was smart and sassy, both

the good kind and the bad of sassy, so you wanted to stay on her good side. She was kind and would do anything for you. She could tease just enough to make you wonder, then pull you back to the truth of the matter before you were done. At what was supposed to be her personal rest time, she provided three or four of us patients with a hot meal—I suspect at her own cost—just before the end of her shift. She was gone with no way to express my gratitude for feeding me.

Vincent—Quietly working through the night, Vincent was unassuming of the burden he carried. For the six patients in his care, the most allowable, everyone got what they needed—vitals taken, medications given, labs, finger pricks [for blood sugar readings], shots—you name it, he seemed on top of the task. He responded when I answered one of his questions with a play on words, saying, "Ah, sense of humor intact." He gently shepherded us through the night when the change of shift released him to the morning.

Ben—Ben announced himself with a booming voice and an apology: "My name is Ben, and I'm here to take care of you today, and I'm sorry for the condition I find you in. We're going to change that starting now." It was at once his self-proclaimed marching order and a sign of hope to each patient. Ben took charge, making a simple, quick org chart, checking everyone's vital statistics, talking to each patient and even delivering us breakfast. Every spirit in the room brightened.

He steadily worked through every task, every wrong he felt needed to be made right. He did enlist the help of one additional RN, Marie, who came from a large OB/GYN clinic nearby. Her clinic staff doctors had taken a vote and decided that half of them would help out in the hospital overrun with virus cases. She said she would be here through March. Marie followed Ben's well-thought out plan which really shook out the tablecloth and reset the table in an orderly manner, doing as he promised in his morning announcement.

While attending to my needs, I asked Ben where we got his training. Expecting the answer "the military," I was surprised to learn it was at Riverside Community Hospital. He expanded on that a bit, about how he got into emergency medicine through a series of better paying job over time. He walked away at one time, working at a nearby Wendy's, but was hired by Kaiser in an on-the-spot-interview. This exchange gave me the opportunity to tell him how much I appreciated his take-charge attitude carried out with compassion and reasonable empathy. It gave us hope and encouragement in a situation where miserable is the most thing one can speak of the dire condition in which we found ourselves.

Aaron—A tall, self-contained man in his early thirties, I first met Aaron on my first night in the circle of hell known as the COVID waiting room. The "room" was a three-sided popup tent where all we did was wait. (More on this side of things later.) Aaron's task was to lead me to the bathroom, the first opportunity to do so in about ten hours. That mean maneuvering me and my wheelchair through a crowded seating area to a portable toilet. He was concerned about the appalling condition of the unit and called EVS[1] before I had completed my business. Despite the mess, it was the best I had felt since arriving at the ER. Aaron squired me back to my waiting position and I waited five more hours before there was another change.

Aaron returned the next night and was the charge nurse in the tent into which I had been moved for treatment. I had been moved to a gurney at 2 am, five hours after Aaron had helped me to the bathroom. It was a far site better and I could stretch out and sleep a little. As Aaron's shift began, he welcomed me with a "Hi, buddy!" acknowledging our acquaintance of the previous night. Finding the conditions greatly improved, he carried on with the task at hand caring for the patients. While not using such a precise method Ben had used, Arron tended each patient with respect, focused medical care and empathy, repeating each test, delivering every dose of medication, and serving each of us with medicines to give us strength.

All of the medical servants do highly repetitive work with an ethic that is the content of their character. All are at war with a virus that leaves the patients they see coughing uncontrollably, feverish, in pain, depressed, and seeking some measure of relief. Who knows what satisfactions and benefits they receive for their difficult work—monetary, sure; caring for others, using their knowledge and expertise, supporting their family, helping our nation through its worse national health crisis in my lifetime. All of the above a scarce measure, I suppose. I only know how grateful I am that each one took care of me.

Blog Entry #2—A Lonely Disease
December 19, 2020

COVID-19 is a very lonely disease. It is happening to you. You are experiencing the loss of control in your lungs. You are making a cough you've

---

1. The hospital's Environmental Services (cleaning).

never felt or heard before. You are the one who has lost the ability to have a normal night's sleep.

COVID-19 is not a very lonely disease. You come to the hospital for help because you know they are helping people there. You've come to seek answers, search the face of these helpers for release from your pain and frustration. You know you need help because that is what they do with suffering people like you.

COVID-19 is a very lonely disease. As you wait, in some cases 8, 10, 12 hours or more, you do a lot of thinking. How did I get here? You consider every option at the length your fevered brain will let you. You ponder every nuance of your life. As your eyes flash across the room at others as sick or worse than you, you see the misery you're in. Your eyes take in the helpers and you pray they stay strong—for you, for others, for what's next.

COVID-9 is not a very lonely disease. If you have one person, a family or friends who care for you, you are not alone. The wider your circle of friends, there is someone concerned, worrying, imagining what you are going through. You are now the person who has COVID-19, and [your experience] is one step closer to [them].

Blog Entry #3—You're the Patient
December 20, 2020

Of course you are; that's why you're here in the hospital and at every moment you are aware that you are the patient. Whether recovering from disease, surgery or injury (there are many reasons to be hospitalized), your job is to be the patient. How could you be otherwise? You don't feel up to anything else. Your energy level is low or non-existent, your breathing is poor or erratic, your thought processes have been scrambled. You are reduced to being a human being and you're grateful for all of the things you *can* do—feed yourself, get to the bathroom (hopefully on time), lie down, cover yourself, rise up after some much needed rest. You can answer questions, make basic requests, and there are brighter moments when your sense of humor kicks in and lightens the mood. None of this changes the fact that you are the patient.

COVID-19 patients have a fair amount of waiting ahead of them. You wait for medicine to come in little paper cups or to be injected into your body—sometimes directly, sometimes via an IV line stuck in your arm unceremoniously early on in your patienthood. You also wait, somewhat less eagerly, for the phlebotomist to draw your blood at an ungodly hour for the day's baseline labs. In an equal but opposite measure of eagerness, you wait [for] your meals. Sometimes you have the opportunity to pre-order your meal choice and wait to see if it comes as requested. With COVID-19, there is no rehabilitation to go to, no physical therapist who comes to you, but you wait in the hope of someone to give you an update on your health. That's why you've had all those tests. The update you're waiting for is, of course, good news of progress toward recovery and health.

The someone you want to hear from most is your doctor. His/her visit is normally once a day and very brief. You're given an update based on the data in your medical chart, not the doctor's personal observations. If you have had the strength and clarity of mind you may have formulated some questions for the doctor and you waited with concern to ask, hoping you don't leave something out of the question and answer session with your doctor and he/she actually listens enough to fully answer you. If something is not quite right, the specter of a new test is on the horizon to rule out an issue or clear a suspicion in the doctor's mind. Of course you want this too, and a bit of waiting for the test and its results are set in motion.

Ultimately, you are waiting for the joyous news that you can go home, but you still might have to wait before that happens. Naturally, you want to be strong enough to go home, feel like going home; you want the going home to mean you're well enough to go home. You're eager to put this behind you, stop being the patient, but apprehensive about all you know is at home. Yes, you want to be better and anticipate you shall be, but how soon? When will you be 100 percent? When will you resume normal functions and actions? More things for which you wait.

Blog Entry #4—The War Zone
December 21, 2020

That's what they called it, emergency rooms dealing with COVID-19 cases like mine. There was a list of emergencies but not much room in the traditional sense. Outside of the ER, a series of popup tents were serving as the "rooms." As I checked in with the ER, it was an area set up for admitting patients where they were taking some information about your medical insurance. I was then set aside to wait for a triage nurse. Since I was in a wheelchair, I could roll from the sunny spot given me to a place in the shade of 8–10 popup tents (see map sketch).

A short while later, I was wheeled to the nurse triage area and my vitals were taken. I was rolled a few feet back to wait for another 10 hours for the next thing to happen. I had arrived at 11:45 am and I watched as the afternoon descended, turning into night. Safety lights came on, street lights came on, space heaters were ignited—none of which dispelled the gloom of despair on the people's faces.

Along about 8:00 pm, I was given an IV, and I asked for a blanket. A rough cotton stadium style blanket [was provided]. I was grateful for the protection as the cold and wind were increasing. The street noise from outside the hospital was also increasing as traffic came and went at the intersection of Valley Blvd. and Sierra Blvd. As the evening wore on, the noise became distracting. You could hear the planes as they approached Ontario Airport. The buses came and went according to their schedule, their air brakes sounding as they stopped nearby. The Union Pacific trains passing a quarter mile away seemed to be just beyond the hospital wall. There was sound from the freeway, speeding cars and hundreds of 18-wheelers thundering by. What I presumed were hot rod cars were peeling away from the traffic light as though in a race—the drivers having invested money in their machines—but showing no concern for the patients. A lot of noise, amplified by the muted darkness inside the War Zone.

Somewhere around 2:00 am, I was moved to the structure in the courtyard called the "noodle." This structure was actually a large, soft-sided tent. Inside, there was room for ten beds, six of which were occupied including me. When I say bed, I mean gurney, but that was better than one of the lounge chair style "beds" that was the option. I knew I would be safe there and could try and get some sleep. It was cold inside, the lights on all the time with no chance of dimming, and a continuous flow of air circulated loudly. [In addition to the gurney, the other advantage to being in the noodle was that I was given oxygen, with frequent tank changes as the oxygen was used up.]

Daylight came and went, but I only left once, at night, to use the portable potty in the courtyard. The following morning, at about 2:30 am, I was tapped to move up. [Despite the oxygen mask, which had slipped off my face, my oxygen saturation level dropped to 70 percent, far below the 93 percent that is standard.] The noodle was still considered an ER room, but with a low O2 saturation level, I was taken inside the [hospital] building and placed in an ER bay.

Nothing was done to me / for me there, other than to put me on a wall unit oxygen port and remove the tank, but I was placed on a nice gurney. Still, the ER staff seemed indifferent to my presence. After just two hours there, I was moved to my actual hospital room. Here I have been cared for well and by kind, compassionate people, the dark brooding despair of the War Zone behind me.

Blog Entry #5—Where Prayer Ends
December 22, 2020

In the solitude of COVID-19, I discovered where prayer ends. Maybe the words are the first thing to go anyway, but they do go away. The most familiar words may come to mind, but they hold no meaning and don't bring comfort. "Thy will be done," always a good prayer, evaporated. "God be merciful to me, a sinner"—may be true but doesn't seem to apply in this void. "Jesus, remember me". . . not yet. Your search for words to string together to express how you feel just ends—no sense of frustration, no remorse, not a bit of embarrassment. The words are just gone.

Deeper in this shadow, you've given up on words, you look for the faces of the people you know who pray. And guess what, they're not there either. My mother taught me to pray—she's gone. I've prayed with dozens of friends and colleagues—I couldn't feel one of you. The further you recess into this abyss, you lose the energy to find a course correction. You get overwhelmed by the bleak terrain you're in. Every "where" seems to lead to a dead end. You can't find the strength to ask, "What's wrong with me?"

In the back of my mind I think of the prayers that are the sighs too deep for words, but I find no comfort there in this dark place of my heart. I recall the hymn, and I quote it to myself:

> "As o'er each continent and island,
> the dawn leads on another day,
> the voice of prayer is never silent,
> nor die the strains of praise away."[2]

Who is praying for me today? My voice is silent. I cannot pray. I don't even want to try. The darkness grow.

---

2. "The Day Thou Gavest, Lord, Is Ended" (v. 3), *The United Methodist Hymnal* #690, one of my favorite hymns.

Beyond these hospital walls, I am told that a world of people are praying for me. Voices from many corners of my life are worried about me, and I am grateful for their concern. I know that prayers are being lifted, and I hope they find a receptive ear in the divine. They need to pray; I can't.

In the non-solitude of COVID-19, I discovered the array of people who are elements in your experience. The nurses are the regulars, tending to your needs, answering your questions, focused on treating you. There are the EVS techs who empty the trash, mop the floors, clean up your spills. Several floors below where you lie [there are] cooks, nutritionists, meal assembly workers, clean-up crews, food deliver people so you get three meals a day.

Closer at hand are the pharmacists, who fulfill prescriptions, provide the dosage cleared by the doctors, so you not only get the therapeutics for your illness, but the daily meds you would be taking at home from Metformin to Lipitor.

Hospital administrators also play their role in hiring qualified staff (at all levels), balancing staff workloads with the demand COVID-19 has made of the health care system. Even in all these roles, the darkness of the pandemic hovers, putting all at risk and challenging the very fabric that you in your darkness as a patient are trying to survive.

Blog Entry #6—Setbacks
December 24, 2020

I suppose with any enterprise there are setbacks. This has certainly been true for me with COVID-19, and it becomes a matter of how you deal with them that gets your through the experience. To rule out the possibility that my recovery was not being prolonged due to a blood clot in my lungs—and I have a history of DVT[3] blood clots—the doctor ordered a CT scan. It would be two days before this was completed.

The first setback was finding someone to put a larger IV into my arm to accommodate the dye contrast they inject into you to do the scan. Without explaining this upfront, the tech was searching for a place to inject the IV needle. On his fourth try, he was successful, but I had to ask him, "Are you in?" Eleven hours had passed since the scan order was placed, and I was hoping this element of progress was a sign things were on the move.

3. DVT = Deep vein thrombosis

For this scan to happen, three more things had to be in place: a wheelchair, an oxygen tank, and a medical transport team to monitor my heart and get me to the scan room. The night passed and nothing more happened. In the fiftieth hour everything converged—in less than a half hour, the scan was accomplished and I was back in bed to await the results of the scan—another 15-hour wait.

These setbacks reveal an overloaded, overwhelmed medical system during peak in the crisis. The bigger setback came when I learned the results of the CT scan. The first course (five doses) of the COVID-19 drug of choice had not done all in could to eliminate the COVID pneumonia from my body. This meant that I was in for an extended hospital stay of at least five more days.

Medically, I understood what this meant and I quickly came to terms with it both emotionally and psychologically. Without being able to breathe on my own, I knew I wasn't ready to go home, nor did I want to go home and [possibly] have to return to the ER. Better stay where you are, have another round of the treatment, and receive the care being given to me.

Maybe setback are life's way of making a pause, re-evaluating, reassessing, revisiting, reviewing where you are and what your next steps are to be. Your life may depend on it.

<u>Blog Entry #7—The Road Not Taken</u>
December 26, 2020

Robert Frost's famous poem, "The Road Not Taken," has been drifting through my mind—especially the part that mentions the dark and deep woods, and the miles to go before I sleep lines.[4] The poem is deceptively simple and more profound the more you ponder it. The fancy word is multivalent. As I rest, I think of the deep darkness I have been experiencing, how over-whelming it has seemed, and what this challenge means to me going forward.

Going forward may seem like words of hope, some level of improvement in my outlook, or some sense of light at the end of the tunnel. Elements of these ideas come to the surface every now and then, but do not linger and disappear as quickly as they arrive. That's where the "miles to go" stakes its claim.

4. The poem is not "The Road Not Taken," but "Stopping by Woods on a Snowy Evening," both by Robert Frost.

When I was first diagnosed as COVID-19 positive, I was determined not to be a statistic [of course, I was already]. Yes, I was one of the new cases among the 52,281 that day; I went on to be one of the 16,426 of hospitalizations. What I did not fathom [was] being one of the 28,538 fatalities from this pandemic. My goal was (and is) to be among those who are the recoveries—again light at the end of the tunnel, but without knowing how long, dark and deep this darkness would be.[5]

Are there other signs I should be noticing? A second round of drugs promises improvement. Better sleep at night is another minor indicator—not without interruptions, but with incremental length and frequency. My appetites is good and even if the food choices are less than ideal for my palette. Repetition may be easy for the kitchen crew, but the tedium of the meals is exasperating. I can understand limited portions, carb and sugar control, calorie counts and many of the elements that make for a controlled diabetic diet. Knowing how slammed the hospital census is gives me a bit of patience and tolerance. Maybe that glimpse into my own minimal compassion is another sign that I am on the mend. Besides, my oxygen saturation level is staying strong with a lowered amount of oxygen being administered. But there are miles to go.

Blog Entry #8—Christmas Day
December 27, 2020

On Christmas Day I received two presents that made the day a bit brighter and unique, even in this situation. The first gift was a bath. I had the presence of mind to plan for it, and I would have done it myself if I hadn't been offered the help I accepted. [While I was seated on the side of the bed, the nurse added warm water to a pouch of pre-soaped sponges; the cleansing solution evaporated on use.[6]]

As the water flowed over my head, I was overcome with emotion. No shame or embarrassment; not helplessness either. What my heart connected to was a faith memory from the 1980's. My mother came to a footwashing service during Holy Week and I washed her feet. Her tears flowed that evening thinking of all the times she had bathed me, and here I was bathing her. In an instant, that memory flooded over me and I wept. The remainder

5. Statistical data from https://covid19.ca.gov/state-dashboard/, accessed January 8, 2021.

6. EasiCleanse bath, no-rinse, self-soaping disposable washcloth by Coloplast.

of that bath produced a deep sense of relief. It had been about 10 days since my last shower.

The second gift of Christmas Day was a slice of cherry pie with a beef tenderloin lunch. It was such a wonderful treat to have a different meal, but the pie proved to be costly. Most patients, repeated the nurses, saw a spike in their blood sugar count, and doses of insulin were required to restored equilibrium.

Feelings of gratitude have begun to surface in the last couple of days. When I have had the strength, opportunity and presence of mind, I have tried to express my gratitude to each nurse, lab tech, EVS or other medical helpers who have assisted me along this journey. In some cases I have witnessed their compassionate care toward others; in other moments I have been the recipient.

When possible, I have complimented their gifts of communication, tender loving care and empathy for the needs of others. Especially in the face of the COVID-19 pandemic, the risks they take and the sacrifices they are making—personally and professionally—cannot be overstated. Gratitude seem such an inadequate word for such an enormous gift.

<u>Blog Entry #9—Medication</u>
December 29, 2020

How did my presents come wrapped this Christmas? Pretty paper and bows did not seem to exist in my mind; boxes, bags and stockings were mere far-off ideas that came and went with the moments. Shopping, wrapping and plans for a Christmas celebration were interrupted by the disease that left no room for preparation.

Early on in my hospitalization, I was given two medications meant to address the COVID-19 pneumonia ravaging my system. At the point they were first given to me, it was simply a matter of acceptance that I was receiving the meds. They were simply described to me as a steroid (Dexamethazone[7]) and a drug developed for viral infections (Remdesivir[8]). I subsequently learned that the steroid's purpose was to open the airways

---

7. Dexamethazone is a corticosteroid the prevents the release of substances in the body that cause inflammation.

8. Remdesivir is an antiviral medication approved for emergency use to treat COVID-19.

in my lungs while the Remdesivir was to counteract the COVID-19 virus specifically.

It wasn't until the second round of Remdesivir treatment that I began to ask questions about the treatment and what I was experiencing. I had a clear sense of hallucinogenic effects for at least one of the drugs. (I was told is not the Remdesivir but the steroid.) Each time I was to receive the drugs, I felt I had to brace myself for their effects.

At the onset of treatment I saw flashes of bright white light, heard loud noises, and I would randomly shout out brief, clear sentences (in my mind) that came out as mumbled words. Later on, I began to think about the medication differently. Rather than brace myself, I began to say, "Let this be a healing balm for my body. Course through my system and cleanse my lungs of this pneumonia. Bring my body rest and recovery; let there be health and wholeness." Those final three treatments were equally challenging, but more tolerable than the first seven had been.

Beyond these disease-specific meds, I was given my usual daily prescriptions and checked for blood sugar (multiple times a day!), given blood thinner (Lovenox) and when necessary, insulin—a protocol that replaced the use of metformin.

Sketch of the War Zone

(See page 52)

Legend

To the east—The exterior Emergency Room wall of the Kaiser hospital building, lined with popup shelters for holding COVID-19 patients; the ER admitting desk is in the lower right corner.

To the south—The curtained area with chairs, inside and out, for COVID patients awaiting treatment.

To the west—Additional popup shelters with chairs for COVID patients awaiting treatment.

To the north—Temporary bathroom facilities for the 85–100 patients awaiting treatment.

Center right—The nurse triage area with 3 or 4 open "bays" for assessing patient needs.

Center left—The Noodle with six patient "rooms" for treatment; includes a storage area and a nurse's station.

> *This map was drawn on a "get to know you" page provided in the new patient packet given when you are admitted to the hospital. Rather than redraw it, this is the original sketch (see Legend on previous page).*

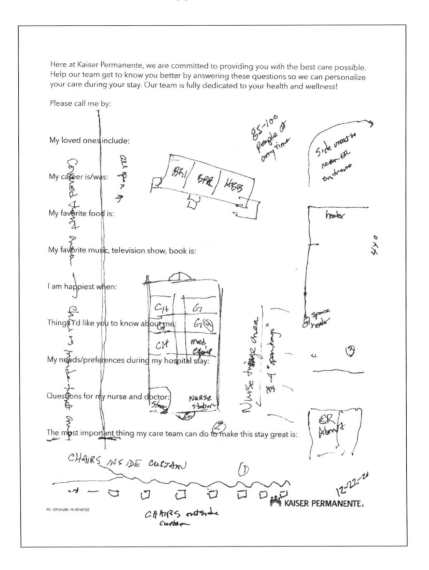

Here at Kaiser Permanente, we are committed to providing you with the best care possible. Help our team get to know you better by answering these questions so we can personalize your care during your stay. Our team is fully dedicated to your health and wellness!

Please call me by:

My loved ones include:

My career is/was:

My favorite food is:

My favorite music, television show, book is:

I am happiest when:

Things I'd like you to know about me:

My needs/preferences during my hospital stay:

Questions for my nurse and doctor:

The most important thing my care team can do to make this stay great is:

NS-10954 (08-19) REVERSE

KAISER PERMANENTE.

Sketch of View from Hospital Window

(See page 83)

(East)
San Bernardino airport and mountains
My home to the east in Redlands

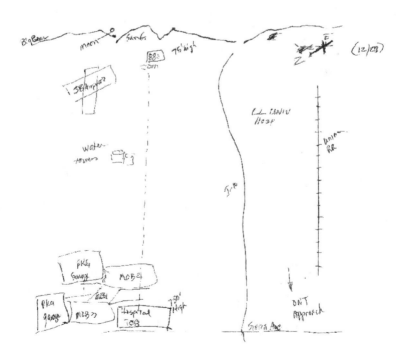

(West)
Kaiser Hospital compound
Union Pacific railyard

Brown "Duck" Illustration

(See page 66)

Bibliography

"Andrea Bocelli: Music for Hope—Live from Duomo di Milano." *Andrea Bocelli*. YouTube video, 24:56. https://www.youtube.com/watch?v=huTUOek4LgU.

Associated Press. "US tops 500,000 virus deaths." https://apnews.com/article/us-over-500ok-coronavirus-deaths-4ffa86c709f6a843de9cf0711e7215cf.

Butler, Judith. "Toward a Shared Space." *Time*, May 3, 2021.

California Department of Public Health. "Blueprint for a Safer Economy." cdph.ca.gov/blueprint.

Centers for Disease Control. https://www.cdc.gov/coronavirus/2019-ncov/index.html.

———, cdc.gov/coronavirus/prevent-getting-sick, accessed June 23, 2021.

Crisp, George. *The Sermon Book (Year A), Sowing in Good Soil*. Middletown, DE: Self-published, 2021.

Dockterman, Eliana. "Ready to Commit?" *Time*, June 7–14, 2021.

Family Service Association of Redlands. redlandsfamilyservice.org.

Fender, Beth, et. al, "A Liturgy for When We Cannot Meet." Franklinville, NJ: The Order of Saint Luke, 2020.

"Former Vice President Joe Biden addresses the coronavirus pandemic– 3/12/2020." *CNBC Television*. YouTube video, 18:44. https://www.youtube.com/watch?v=2QOidd8FGUM.

Freeman, John, "A New Narrative." *Time*, April 26-May 3, 2021.

French, David, "Can We Escape the Vaccine Culture War." *Time*, June 21–28, 2021.

Frost, Robert. "Stopping by Woods on a Snowy Evening."

Ghebreyesus, Tedros Adhanom. "Opening Remarks at the Media Briefing." *World Health Organization*. https://www.who.int/director-general/speeches.

Health.com. "What is PPE?" health.com/condition/infectious-diseases/coronavirus/what-is-ppe.

Li, Wei. "Racial Disparities in COVID-19." *Science in the News: Harvard University Graduate School of Arts and Sciences*, October 24, 2020, sitn.hms.harvard.edu.

Lipman, Joanne. "The Pandemic Revealed How Much We Hate Our Jobs. Now We Have a Chance to Reinvent Work." *Time*, June 14, 2021.

Bibliography

Melvin, Craig. "Yusef Salaam Of Exonerated Central Park Five Shares His Story" *Today.* Youtube video, 5:09. May 18, 2021. https://www.youtube.com/watch?v=9YAu5ivb5x0.

Merriam-Webster. s.v. "pandemic." https://www.merriam-webster.com/dictionary/pandemic.

National Institutes of Health. COVID patient "Treatment Guidelines," December 12, 2020, accessed May 25, 2021.

National Public Radio. "In wave after deadly wave, COVID has claimed 1 million lives in the U.S." March 31, 2021. https://www.npr.org/sections/health-shots/2022/05/17/1093651037/us-one-million-deaths.

———. "Timeline: How Trump Has Downplayed The Coronavirus Pandemic." October 2, 2020. https://www.npr.org/sections/latest-updates-trump-covid-19-results/2020/10/02/919432383/how-trump-has-downplayed-the-coronavirus-pandemic.

Park, Alice. "Decoding COVID-19." *Time,* May 10–17, 2021.

Redlands Charitable Resource Coalition. rcrchelp.com, accessed July 1, 2021.

Redlands Daily Facts. December 29, 2021, A-1.

Schafer, Cole. *Honey Copy.* "Being good at things isn't the point of doing them." https://www.honeycopy.com/copywritingblog/kurt-vonnegut-advice, accessed August 13, 2021.

Taylor, Derrick Bryson. "Is the Coronavirus an Epidemic or a Pandemic? It Depends on Who's Talking." *The New York Times,* March 11, 2020. https://nytimes.com/2020/02/28/health/coronavirus-pandemic-epidemic.html

Thomas, Debie. "My Mother's Gift of Words." *Christian Century,* June 2, 2021.

The United Methodist Hymnal. Nashville, TN: United Methodist Publishing House, 1989.

"Tracking COVID-19 in California." State of California Government. https://covid19.ca.gov/state-dashboard/.

Webster's Ninth New Collegiate Dictionary. Springfield, MA: Merriam-Webster Inc., Publishers, 1987.

World Health Organization. "COVID-19: China." https://www.who.int/emergencies/disease-outbreak-news/item/2020-DON229, December 31, 2019.

Yale Medicine. "Our Pandemic Year—A COVID Timeline." https://www.yalemedicine.org/news/covid-timeline.